ANNA AKHMATOVA
SELECTED POEMS

ANNA AKHMATOVA

Selected Poems

Translated by Richard McKane

BLOODAXE BOOKS

Copyright © Richard McKane 1969, 1989
translations and introduction.

ISBN: 1 85224 063 6

First published 1989 by
Bloodaxe Books Ltd,
P.O. Box 1SN,
Newcastle upon Tyne NE99 1SN.

Bloodaxe Books Ltd acknowledges
the financial assistance of Northern Arts.

891.7
A 315 se
1989

ACKNOWLEDGEMENTS
Acknowledgements are due to VAAP for Akhmatova poems
first published since 1973. Some of these translations have
appeared before, in earlier versions, in *Selected Poems of Anna
Akhmatova*, translated by Richard McKane (Penguin Books and
Oxford University Press, 1969); in *The Penguin Book of Post
War Russian Poetry* (1974), *The Shalford Book of 20th Century
Russian Poetry* (Kozmik Press, 1985), and *The Penguin Book of
Women Poets* (1978); and in the magazines *The Alchemist,
Malahat Review* and *Zenos*.

Cover portrait by K. Petrov-Vodkin (1922).

Frontispiece by Elizabeth McKane.

Typesetting by E.F. Peterson & Son, South Shields.

Printed in Great Britain by
Bell & Bain Limited, Glasgow, Scotland.

For Elizabeth McKane

Contents

17 Introduction
30 Translator's Note and Acknowledgements

35 *Briefly About Myself* by Anna Akhmatova
39 *Fragments from Memoirs* by Anna Akhmatova

FROM EVENING

50 'The pillow'
50* 'I couldn't get to sleep'
51 The Grey-Eyed King
51 Love
52 'The boy who plays the bagpipes'
52 'In the memory the sun grows dimmer'
53 'The door is half open'
54 Song of the Last Meeting
55 'You suck my soul'
55* In the Forest
56 'I live like a cuckoo in a clock'
56 'He loved three things'
57 'Today they brought no letter'
57 Garden
58 White Night

FROM ROSARY

60 To M. Lozinsky
60 'I taught myself to live simply'
61 Sleeplessness
61 'I have come to replace you, sister'
62 In the Evening
63 'We shall not drink from the same glass'
64 'I have a certain smile'
64 'Evening hours at the table'
65 'I know, I know, the skis'
65 The Visitor
66 To Alexander Blok

FROM WHITE FLOCK

68   'The blue varnish of the sky dims'
68   'I will leave your white house'
68*   'The fir wood is white'
69   'A black twisted road'
70   'I see, I see the crescent moon'
70   'He was jealous, worried and tender'
71   'How can you look at the Neva'
71   Parting
72   'The seaside garden road is dark'
72   'Frosty sun'
73   '"Tall woman where is your gipsy boy"'
74   'We thought: we're poor'
74   To N.G. Chulkova
75   Dream
75   'I still see hilly Pavlovsk'
76   '"Coorlee, coorlee!" The cranes call'
77   'You cannot get here'
77   'The Immortelle is pink'
78   'Everything promised him to me'
78   'One memory lies within me'
79   'The town vanished'
79   'It seems that the voice of man'
80   'Yes I loved those gatherings'

FROM WAYSIDE GRASS

82   'How terribly my body changed'
82   'A string of small beads'
83   'O God, I can forgive everything done against me'
83   'The world's fame is like smoke'
83   'I'd have thought you might come into my dreams less'
84   'You looked into my face'
84   'And I alone remained'
85   'I will not speak to anyone'
85   'I did not draw the curtains'
86   'This meeting has been sung by no one'
86   'I waited in vain for him'
87   'Both of us so quiet now'
87   'When the news finally reaches him'
88   'So now farewell, my Petersburg'
89   'To wake up at dawn'

89	'I walked with a light step'
89	'Suddenly it became quiet in the house'
90	'There is a troubled, uneasy hour'
90	'Oh no, burnt by a sweet fire'
91	'I don't like flowers'
92	'It's simple'
92	'The river flows without hurry'
93	'For a whole day'
93	'When the people waited'
94	'Now no one will listen to songs and poems'
94	At Night
95	'When the moon does not roam'
95	'I asked the cuckoo'
96	'Why is this century worse'

FROM ANNO DOMINI

98	Lullaby
98	Little Song
99	'A blackened and twisted log bridge'
100	'You thought I was that type'
101	'Terror, rummaging through things in the dark'
101	'A pine bedstead'
101	Slander
102	Black Dream
105	'I am not among those who left our land'
106	'The swans are carried on the wind'
106	'If only I could fall ill in earnest'
107	Biblical Poems
110	'That fantastic autumn'
110	'It is good here'
111	New Year Ballad
111*	'The ale is brewed'
112*	To Many

FROM REED

114	Inscription in a Book (To M.L. Lozinsky)
114	The Muse
115	To the Artist
115*	'One can leave this life so simply'
116*	'Forgive me that I'm coping badly'
116	'Here Pushkin's exile began'

116   'If the moon's horror splashes'
117   'That city that I have loved'
118   Couplet
118   Incantation
118*   'Wild honey'
119*   'Why did you poison the water'
119   'Didn't he send a swan for me'
120   'Some mirror themselves in lovers' eyes'
121   'I hid my heart from you'
121   Boris Pasternak
122   Voronezh
123   Dante
123*   A Little Geography
124*   Fragments of Pottery
125*   Imitation of the Armenian
126   'Celebrate this, our last anniversary'
126*   'I know there's no moving'
127*   'Happy New Year!'
127*   The Cellar of Memory
128*   'For all those'
129   Cleopatra
129*   Stanzas
130*   'I put my curly-haired son to bed'
131*   'So the dark souls fly off'
132   'When a man dies'
132   Willow
133*   'The neighbour woman, out of pity'
133*   'So in defiance'
134   Splitting Up
135   Mayakovsky in 1913
135   Inscription in the Book *Wayside Grass*
136   Leningrad in March 1941

FROM SEVENTH BOOK

The Secrets of the Craft

139   The Secrets of the Craft
144   'In books I always like the last page'
145   Pushkin
145   'Our sacred craft has existed'
145   In 1940

Wind of War

149   Wind of War
154*   'Anyone can do what I am doing'
155*   'Let us go now to Samarkand
155*   From the Tashkent Notebook
155   Death
157   The Moon in the Zenith
162   'When the moon lies on the windowsill'
163   Tashkent Breaks into Blossom
163   'It was your lynx eyes, Asia'
164*   Inscribed on the Poem
164*   'I am what I am'
165*   'You like to call to the tomtit'
166*   'The double hides his Bourbon profile'
166*   'I would not have seen the quince flower bloom'
167   From the Plane
168*   Lament
168   Liberated
169*   'Distant delineations of Faust'
169*   'He, whom the people mockingly called King'
170*   'With the lads in the gutter'

*   *   *

173   'One takes the straight line'
173   Youth
174   Smolensk Graveyard
175   Hearthwarming
176   Three Autumns
177   Near Kolomna
178   'All the souls of the dear ones'
178*   'Everyone went away'
179   The Last Return
180   'The man who means nothing to me now'
180*   'I do not have any special claim'
180*   'Others take their loved ones with them'
181*   'It is no wonder that my unruly poems'
181*   'In vain you cast at my feet'
182*   'They will forget'
183*   'So I have no flight out'
183*   Inscribed in a Book
184*   Heiress
184*   'What does parting mean to us'

185*   To the Poem
185*   Prologue
186   A String of Quatrains
188   Second Anniversary
189   Inscription on a Portrait
189   Cinque
191   The Sweetbriar in Bloom (From a Burnt Notebook)
198   From the *Burnt Notebook Cycle*
199   Midnight Verses
203   Moscow Trefoil
204   'That fruitbearing autumn'
204   On Not Sending the Poem

Uneven

206   Sonnet by the Sea
206   Music
207   Drawing in a Book of Poems
207   Fragment
207   Summer Garden
208   'Don't frighten me'
209   To Pushkin's Town
210   Little Songs
212   From the Cycle of Tashkent Pages
213*   'You live on, but I won't live long'
214*   'Distance collapsed in rubble'
214*   'There's a voice outside the door'
214   March Elegy
215*   Speed
215*   'These praises do not become me'
216   Echo
216*   Masquerade Chatter
217   Three Verses
218*   'I was wrongly captivated'
218*   'We did not face the disasters together in vain'
219*   *From* Black Songs
220*   'Under the most sacred maple'
220*   Listening to Singing
221   A Page of Ancient History
222   'Those "unforgettable dates" have come round'
222*   Petersburg in 1913
223*   'If everyone in the world'
223   Tsarskoye Selo Ode

225   Our Own Land
226   The Last Rose
226*   A Wreath for the Dead
232   Twenty-three years later
233   In Memory of V.S. Sreznevskaya
233*   The North
234*   Christmas Eve
234*   From an Italian Diary
234*   Imitation of the Korean
235   In Vyborg
235*   Fragment
236*   'The ice grows thick on the windowpanes'
236*   'No, we are not playing'
237*   'The strange companion was sent to me from hell'
237*   Couplets
238   On the Road

A HALF CENTURY OF QUATRAINS

240   'A Half Century of Quatrains'

EPIC AND DRAMATIC FRAGMENTS

248   Epic Motifs
251   Northern Elegies
258   *From* 'Prologue': A Play
263*   The Big Confession

LONG POEMS

268   By the Sea Shore
276   The Way of All the Earth
281   Requiem: Poems 1935–1940
287   Poem Without a Hero

315   *Anna Akhmatova's Note to Poem Without a Hero*
319   *Libretto for ballet of Poem Without a Hero*

322   *Translator's Notes to the Poems*
337   *Envoi*

ANNA AKHMATOVA, 1940

Introduction

This Introduction omits many of the biographical details covered by Anna Akhmatova in *Briefly About Myself* and *Fragments from Memoirs*, which follow my piece. Akhmatova's own Note to *Poem Without a Hero* and the Ballet Libretto to *Poem Without a Hero* are included at the back of the book.

I.

At one stage Anna Akhmatova was contemplating a long autobiographical prose work, which she said would be a 'cousin' to the prose works *Safe Conduct* by Boris Pasternak and *The Noise of Time* by Osip Mandelstam. We have the framework, and indeed several fragments which would have gone into such an 'autobiography' are translated here, but it was never written. Akhmatova was not only a poet, and an authority on Pushkin, but also, at times *faute de mieux*, a translator, and an epigrammatic conversationalist. The poems which are nearest to her conversation, as Nadezhda Mandelstam has remarked, are her Quatrains. Fortunately for us we have a faithful record of her conversations with Lydia Chukovskaya in the 40s and 50s, which we find recorded in her two books about Akhmatova: a third is in preparation. These books are being translated and published in English by Collins in 1990. With all their massive apparatus on the poems, the English-speaking reader will soon be able to share the insights of one of Akhmatova's most faithful friends.

Nadezhda Mandelstam in *Hope Against Hope* and *Hope Abandoned* and to a lesser extent *Third Book* (the latter as yet unpublished in English), gives a mine of information on Akhmatova's character and poetry, and her deep love for the two Mandelstams. Since these first two Memoirs are widely available in Penguin Books, I will not extract from them the relevant passages, but urge the reader to turn to them. The *Third Book* shows a kinship between Akhmatova and her exact contemporary T.S. Eliot, which is, elsewhere, further developed in a book on Akhmatova by her friend, and one time literary secretary, the poet Anatoly Naiman, to be published in English in 1991 by Peter Halban Publishers.

This fuller collection of Anna Akhmatova's poetry, which includes new translations of the poems of the Stalinist terror, some of which (especially *Fragments of Pottery*) Akhmatova

17

almost included in *Requiem*, should be read as a companion document to Osip Mandelstam's works, Boris Pasternak's, and to a lesser extent perhaps Marina Tsvetayeva's – thus, with herself, making 'There are Four of Us' of Akhmatova's 1961 poem (p.230).

But there are other poets whose poems or personalities inter-related with Anna Akhmatova. Certainly Innokenty Annensky ('The Master', see *A Wreath for the Dead*, pp.226–32) was an enormous creative influence on her, that she frequently acknow-ledged and has been further pointed out to me by David McDuff, the expert on Annensky and translator of *Marina Tsvetayeva: Selected Poems* (Bloodaxe Books, 1987).

Nikolai Gumilyov and Akhmatova wrote poems to each other, and some of these have been documented in English in Amanda Haight's excellent biography *Anna Akhmatova: A Poetic Pil-grimage* (Oxford University Press, 1976). He was Akhmatova's husband for eight years (1910–18) during which they were often separated, and the founder of the poets' movement Acmeism. Acmeism is briefly discussed by Akhmatova in one of her fragments, where she indicates that it was a reaction against Symbolism, the proponents of which were Alexander Blok and Vyacheslav Ivanov. Vyacheslav Ivanov had poetry readings at his famous 'Tower', which both Akhmatova and Mandelstam attended. However, perhaps these occasions at the 'Tower' (described to me by one Russian friend as 'more tea and cakes and dancing for the young') should not be over-solemnised. Mikhail Lozinsky, the poet and translator of Dante and Shakespeare, was also an Acmeist. Akhmatova and Mandelstam (who in the 1930s defined Acmeism as 'A longing for world culture') remained faithful to it all their lives. In his essay *About the Nature of the Word* (published in 1922) Osip Mandelstam had said: 'Acmeism arose out of repulsion: "Away with Symbolism, long live the living rose!" ... Acmeism did not adopt a world view; it brought in a series of new taste sensations, much more valuable than ideas; mostly the taste for an integral literary representation, the image, in a new organic conception.' (*Osip Mandelstam: Selected Essays*, translated by Sidney Monas [University of Texas Press]).

Of the Futurists, working in that movement which has a parallel in the West (whereas Acmeism would seem not to), Velimir Khlebnikov, rather than Vladimir Mayakovsky, seems to have been important to Akhmatova (Lydia Chukovskaya men-tions her positive reactions to reading him). There are echoes of his poem 'Moon Horror' in 'The Cellar of Memory' (p.127; see also Notes) which show that poem is about the Bohemian Cabaret at The Stray Dog Café in the Petersburg of the 1910s. This Cabaret was the scene for what would now be described as performance poetry and drama and dance. The Stray Dog is especially prominent in the Libretto for *Poem Without a Hero*.

Critics (especially Timenchik) have written about Mikhail Kuzmin's possible influence through his *The Trout Breaks the Ice* on the stanza form and material in *Poem Without a Hero*, and Kuzmin had written the Introduction to Akhmatova's first book *Evening*. He plays a sinister role *vis à vis* the dragoon and minor poet Vsevolod Knyazev in *Poem Without a Hero* (and the Libretto). Akhmatova did however seem to like his poetry, which is now being republished in Russian in the West.

Boris Pasternak played a vital role in Anna Akhmatova's life. She wrote with great brevity and insight about him in the prose fragments and dedicated a poem to him in 1936, and three poems which became incorporated in *A Wreath for the Dead*. Simultaneously the realistic value she placed on his friendship was a paramount factor in her life – although she was convinced that he did not read Mandelstam's poetry, and did not seem to be able to digest others' poems, even her own.

Marina Tsvetayeva, whom Akhmatova met only once, in 1940, but whose poems to her, written in 1916, she carried with her wherever she went, enters Akhmatova's poems in 'I am what I am' (p.164) (written in Tashkent), 'There are Four of Us' (p.230) and 'Late Answer' (p.228) and in the tiny prose fragment (p.45). I have been struck by the contrast between the linguistic fireworks of Tsvetayeva, which are almost untranslatable, and Akhmatova's structures, which are classical in the best sense. In my translations I ensured that the essence of each poem and the emotion behind the language was preserved and therefore communicated, whereas I consciously abandoned aspects such as rhyme, rhythm and metre. Somehow, although I abandoned the formal aspects of their poetry in my translation, the subject matter and emotion behind the language got across. Joseph Brodsky in his essay on Akhmatova, *The Keening Muse*, in *Less Than One* (Penguin Books) has mentioned the 'one-dimensionality' of Akhmatova in English translation. My belief, though, is that the richness of the subject matter and the rhythm of the sequence of ideas (which is more important to the English than rhythm and rhyme) can be communicated. To attempt a patterning of the form of the original Russian is, in my view, something to be done in original poetry rather than in translation.

Anna Akhmatova says that her memories of Alexander Blok, the great Symbolist poet of the turn of the century, and author of the apocalyptic *The Twelve* and 'The Scythians', could be put on one page, although her memoir of him in 'Pages from a Diary' (in those days there could be no diaries, Nadezhda Mandelstam comments) is a few pages longer. He was said, by gossip, to be romantically involved with Akhmatova – even down to 'identification' as the King in 'The Grey-Eyed King' (p.51), although he was to live for another ten years. He did however play a significant role in her writing, and starting writing poetry, as can be seen from the couplet 'To A.A. Blok': 'You brought me fear / and the ability to write poetry' (Spring 1914).

In her 'Three Verses' (1944–60) Blok is called the 'tenor of the epoch', a word which apart from its double resonance recalls Blok's words to Akhmatova 'We are not the tenor'. Joseph Brodsky, in an interview in Russian with Solomon Volkov in *Kontinent* (no.53) indicates that the tenor Akhmatova had in mind may have been the Evangelist from Bach's St Matthew Passion – Blok's age having been dominated by Chaliapin's bass voice – and I have inserted his name into the translation along with 'the ineffable swan' Pavlova in *Poem Without a Hero*.

Of the Western authors, Dante must rate as one of the most influential. Both Anna Akhmatova and Osip Mandelstam started reading him in the original at the same time in the 30s. The fact is, though, that their fellow Acmeist Mikhail Lozinsky was doing in the 30s a translation of *The Divine Comedy*. His translation is the best I have read in any language, and was a heroic labour, for he was suffering from the terrible disease of elephantiasis. Akhmatova's moving Memoir to him and her poem to him 'Inscription in a Book' (p.114) are evidence of their long friendship. She also wrote short memoirs of Blok, Mandelstam and Modigliani, who did several portraits of her when she was in Paris in 1910, only one of which survives.

Similarly Shakespeare, whom Anna Akhmatova read in the original, was a double influence through Boris Pasternak's (and Lozinsky's) translations. We see his vital importance in 'To the Londoners' from the Cycle *In 1941*, where Hamlet, Julius Caesar and King Lear are models for vicarious horror and suffering at a time when the whole of Europe was suffering a worse horror than Shakespeare's. One remembers the insistence of crowds at readings by Pasternak (and Akhmatova) that Pasternak should read Shakespeare's Sonnet 66 ('Tired with all these for restful death I cry'). 'Vicarious' is perhaps too light a word to apply to such realism as Shakespeare's – or Akhmatova's. I have it on the authority of a Russian friend that *Macbeth* was very much on her mind when she was writing *Requiem*. An actual direct translation from Shakespeare is in the *Requiem* poem 'To Death' (p.285): the 'poison'd shot' (of the informer) for what is normally translated as a 'poison gas shell'. This is an example of the nuggets of information contained in Anatoly Naiman's work.

It is my belief that the Akhmatova poems of the 30s and 40s will become the texts of poetry under repression. Whether *glasnost* continues or not in the Soviet Union, and whether or not repression of a different quality to its Soviet counterpart develops in the West, Akhmatova's poems will be read as documentary evidence: perhaps as Osip Mandelstam put it in his *Poem/ Oratorio to the Unknown Soldier*, 'in judgement of the judge and witness'. Anna Akhmatova, and indeed Nadezhda Mandelstam, were both Christians, and perhaps not enough has been said about Anna Akhmatova's Christian poetics of suffering.

Four figures who are alive today who knew Anna Akhmatova, from Isaiah Berlin, to Lydia Chukovskaya, to Joseph Brodsky, to Anatoly Naiman, describe an immense, almost regal, dignity. Her personal dignity did not only emerge from her noble family life in Tsarskoye Selo, but also from her stance as a poet. She had an august presence even in the depths of poverty (which lasted most of her life). According to Nadezhda Mandelstam, Akhmatova was given an old age pension, enough to keep her in cigarettes and matches, at the age of 35, while Mandelstam (that other 'old' poet) was given a pension at the same age 'for services to Russian literature and in view of the impossibility of finding employment for the writer in Soviet literature', yet they and their poetry were younger and longer-lived than the age. Akhmatova's imposing dignity was borne out in the ceremony for the Honorary Oxford Doctorate, presented in Oxford in 1965, the year before she died.

Akhmatova was married to the poet Nikolai Gumilyov in 1910, after a four year engagement, which she later claimed burned out her marriage. By this time she had adopted the *nom de plume* Akhmatova. She decided to write under a pseudonym after an outburst of anger from her father, who said that by publishing the poems she had written she would bring shame to the family name of Gorenko. 'Akhmatova' became not just the poet's *nom* de plume, but the name with which she signed her legal documents. She never adopted Gumilyov's surname, or those of her subsequent husbands Shileyko and Punin. She had chosen the Tatar name Akhmatova because it had been her great-grandmother's. She describes it in one of her Quatrains:

My Name

Tatar, dense textured,
came from nowhere,
sticks to any disaster,
in fact it is disaster.

Of the contemporary prose writers who influenced Akhmatova, Mikhail Bulgakov, the author of *Master and Margarita*, and Zoshchenko, the satirist, were close to her, and are remembered in *A Wreath for the Dead*. Zoshchenko was singled out with her by the second decree against Akhmatova in 1946. The first decree of the Central Committee in 1925, which was never fully publicised and the existence of which came as a surprise to the editors of the Western Edition in 1966 — goes a long way to explain the period of non-publication of poetry, wrongly described as 'silence', when Akhmatova turned to the architecture of St Petersburg and wrote several studies on Pushkin. It should be noted that her two great friends, Boris Pasternak and Osip Mandelstam, both had periods to which few poems can be ascribed. The period, from 1923 to 1936, which was also a difficult one for her personally, served, so to speak, to build up steam, and its vindication lies in the superb poetry, very different from her earlier poems, that boiled over to culminate in the year 1940, when she finished *Requiem*, began *Poem Without a Hero*, and wrote *The Way of All Earth*, besides many other powerful lyrics.

Zoshchenko and Akhmatova were singled out for attack in a decree of 14 August 1946 in *Pravda*. The Central Committee ordered the magazine *Leningrad* to cease publication, severely reprimanded *Zvezda*, and ordered that they should have nothing to do with Akhmatova and Zoshchenko. The attack on Akhmatova was reinforced by the personal intervention of Zhdanov, who was tipped as the possible successor to Stalin. Akhmatova's themes of love and religion were peculiarly vulnerable to attack from Zhdanov, who demanded that literature serve the state. He claimed that 'mists of loneliness and hopelessness alien to Soviet literature run through the whole history of Akhmatova's "crea-

22

tive" work'. Zhdanov used Akhmatova and Zoshchenko as scapegoats and his treatment of them was calculated to stamp out any opposition among the intelligentsia. Amanda Haight in her biography recounts how Akhmatova met Zoshchenko in the street at a time when he had heard of the decree but Akhmatova had not. Akhmatova, bewildered at Zoshchenko's statements, only realised the full horror of the situation when she read the newspaper (wrapped around the fish she had queued for at the fishmongers). In September 1946 both Akhmatova and Zoshchenko were expelled from the Writer Union. Under *glasnost* in October 1988 the Decree of 1946 against Akhmatova and Zoshchenko and their expulsion from the Union of Writers were rescinded.

It was Osip Mandelstam who pointed to Akhmatova's 'genesis in Russian prose': 'Akhmatova brought to the Russian lyric the wealth of the Russian novel of the nineteenth century.' The psychological balance of her poems owes much to Dostoyevsky, and some of the psychologised landscapes of St Petersburg draw on Gogol and Dostoyevsky. Mandelstam also says in his essay *Storm and Stress*: 'Akhmatova, using the purest literary language of her time, adapted with extraordinary steadfastness the traditional devices of Russian folksong, and not only Russian, but folksong in general.' And one of the major elements of folksong is the lament, which Akhmatova was able to employ in the personal and the patriotic, and to make it and the art of memorialisation her trademark.

Mandelstam himself, who was among the many poets who wrote poems to Akhmatova – indeed the poems written to her would fill a volume – was a close friend and fellow poet. He received the respect from Akhmatova which she accorded to the great dead poets, who lived for her. She suffered for him and for Nadezhda when they were in exile in Voronezh, and wrote a poem after visiting him, and she intervened on his behalf on many occasions. When he died on the way to labour camp in Vladivostok, probably on 27 December 1938, she marked that date two years later in her *Poem Without a Hero*. She became one of the preservers of his heritage.

Alexander Pushkin, to whom Akhmatova dedicated a brilliant little poem (p.146), was a passion for Akhmatova. In the 20s and early 30s she wrote several studies of Pushkin, which were eventually published and form the greater part of her prose work. He must have been a solace to her in those times, as he has been to millions of Russians over the years. It is fitting that Anna Akhmatova represents the 'True Twentieth Century' – whether as its conscience, or as a woman of great strength and powers – just as Pushkin represented the 19th century. Of all the 20th century Russian writers, Anna Akhmatova is the most uniting.

One of the features of Akhmatova's last years was that she attracted to herself, as a witness of the age, many readers and visitors as well as poets and writers.

In the Russian magazine *Vremya i My* (1987, no.97), Joseph Brodsky says (in my translation): 'The simple fact that this woman forgave her enemies was the best lesson for a young man, like your obedient servant, a lesson that is the essence of Christianity. We very rarely talked about poems as such. She always showed us everything she wrote – I was not the only one – there were four of us – Rein, Naiman, Bobyshev and I. She called us "the magical choir/chorus". She always showed us her poems and translations, but there was no piousness, no fawning.' These four Leningrad poets and others seemed to give her that companionship and *ésprit* that she had certainly lacked at times in her life. These meetings often took place at her *dacha* in Komarovo, which she had been given in her last years by the Writers' Union – one of the few "perks" she had in her life. In another interview in Russian in *Kontinent* (no.55), Akhmatova's friend Joseph Brodsky says: 'Akhmatova, with just the tone of her voice or a turn of her head, turned you into "homo sapiens".' Her wonderful deep voice was captured in a recording by Peter Norman of her reading *Requiem* in that voice full of suffering. For the first time, hearing her read that poem, I realised that *her voice* was a better translation for the Russian word *toska* – more anguish than longing, and more longing than anguish – than any dictionary definition.

II.

Her stay in evacuation in Tashkent (1941–44) brought into her poetry the Asian themes that her Genghisite name implied (Akhmatova was descended from the last Khan of the Golden Horde – see her *Fragments from Memoirs*), and the Tashkent poems add a dimension to Anna Akhmatova's poems equivalent to the role of Armenia in Osip Mandelstam's poetry, and Georgia in Pasternak's and Iranian themes in Velimir Khlebnikov's poetry.

But Akhmatova's landscapes or cityscapes are Petersburg – Tsarskoye Selo, Leningrad – Pushkin's town, and to a lesser extent the Crimea (Sebastopol), Slepnyovo (the Gumilyovs' family estate, where Lev Gumilyov, Akhmatova's son, was brought up by his grandmother), Moscow, and in the final years, Komarovo, on the Karelian isthmus, 50 kilometres from Leningrad, where Akhmatova had a *dacha*. The presence of St Petersburg/Petrograd/Leningrad, whose architecture she studied in the 20s and 30s, was infused for her with Dostoyevsky and Pushkin. Sharon Leiter has made a whole study of this theme in her book *Akhmatova's Petersburg* (Cambridge University Press).

Tsarskoye Selo plays an enormous part in Anna Akhmatova's poetry – so great that Marina Tsvetayeva calls her 'The Muse of Tsarskoye Selo' in one of her poems. Akhmatova herself in one version of 'Tsarskoye Selo Ode' included a biting comment of her third husband N. Punin as an epigraph: 'You are a poet of local, Tsarskoye Selo significance.' She lived there from the age of one to sixteeen (with summers on the Black Sea) and in later years. Situated close to St Petersburg, the Royal Village, as the name could be translated, was Pushkin's village, and where Annensky taught classical languages and was a headmaster. It included the Tsar's Summer Palace, and the Yekaterinsky Sad (Catherine the Great's Garden) which had a lake, and formal gardens with statuary. Also near Petersburg, Pavlovsk with its 'Railway Station', where concerts were held, also figures in her poetry.

Although Akhmatova did not live in Moscow for extended periods she had good friends there – especially the Ardovs. Indeed, Moscow was extremely important for her, although in a different way to Leningrad. Joseph Brodsky, in the *Kontinent* interview with Solomon Volkov has described the process of 'Akhmatovka', which happened in her last years, where guest after guest was received by Akhmatova. In the 50s she regularly visited her friend Boris Pasternak outside Moscow in his *dacha* at Peredelkino. They shared a Christian faith and view of suffering.

Akhmatova was evacuated by plane from Leningrad by special order after the blockade had started in 1941, and then made her way overland to Chistopol, near Yelabuga in the Ukraine, where Marina Tsvetayeva hanged herself that August. Akhmatova then went to Tashkent, where there were other writers' families, after making a long detour by train through Siberia, which showed her more of Russia than she had ever seen before, and which made a deep impression on her. In Tashkent ('*Constantinople pour les pauvres*'), after staying in a room where Mikhail Bulgakov's widow had been living (see 'Hearthwarming', p.175), she lived for a time in a *balakhan* or attic with Nadezhda Mandelstam. Here she composed the play *E nu me Elish*, which she later burned, but fragments of which she reconstituted into *Prologue (A Tragedy or Dream within a Dream)* and *The Big Confession*. The return trip to Moscow *en route* for Leningrad prompted a poem whose original variant shows her indignation at being abandoned by Garshin. Garshin was a close friend who had formerly wanted to marry her (though on the difficult condition that she should take his surname). When she was evacuated to Tashkent he stayed on in Leningrad during the blockade. Akhmatova believed that this affected the balance of his mind.

The conscious decision that she had taken before 1917 to remain in Russia with her homeland did not stop her critics from tarring her with the brush of 'emigration'. She was even labelled an 'internal emigré'. The Second World War had given Russian writers a respite: the external German threat had temporarily quashed the threats from within. Akhmatova rose to the occasion with some superb poetry which was patriotic not only in its sentiments to the Russian people but also in its loyalty to the Russian language. The poems of *Wind of War* include 'In Memory of a Friend' (1945), which Peter Levi has said 'seems to be made of nothing, yet no other poem in any language commemorates that time so well or touches one so deeply.'

In November 1945 Akhmatova met by chance Isaiah Berlin, the Oxford philosopher, then attached to the British Embassy in Moscow as a First Secretary. He happened to ask about Akhmatova in a bookshop while on a short trip to Leningrad, and was put in touch with her by the owner. She agreed to see him. At that time Russian citizens were practically never allowed contact with foreigners. In fact Isaiah Berlin was only the second foreigner Anna Akhmatova had met in decades – the first being Jozef Czapski, the Polish officer she met in Tashkent during the War, who is the subject of the the poem 'From Tashkent Pages'. Sir Isaiah Berlin, in his book *Personal Impressions* (Oxford University Press), has described his two meetings with Akhmatova in 1945–46, their phone call on his 1956 visit and their final meeting in Oxford, with great detail and sensitivity. The deep impression he made on her led to the Cycles *Cinque* (p.189), *The Sweetbriar Blooms* (p.191), *Midnight Verses* (p.199) and other short poems indicated in the Notes, and moreover the Third Dedication and other lines in *Poem Without a Hero*. Although no direct mention of him is made in Soviet editions, he has become 'a Myth' in Russia, a myth, moreover, for 'people in the know'. Stalin himself was furious on hearing of their meetings. But the wave (perhaps the seventh wave) of air that Isaiah Berlin brought into that room in Fountain House in the Sheremetev Palace in that winter buoyed up Akhmatova for years, and in different ways these two great characters bore the responsibility for what Sir Isaiah Berlin described to me as 'that *tactless* meeting' (my italics), although their interpretations of the meeting's significance in personal, poetic, mythological and global terms, seem to me to be completely different.

The linkage of poems, events and arrests in a Russia of such random terror, poverty and grinding depression as those of Stalin's times, documented by Akhmatova in *Requiem*, and other poems, can only be sought in a will that the truth must survive, even if the people perished. Anna Akhmatova's earlier poetry had shown her to be capable not so much of romanticism, as of a 'pining' (*tomlenie*) which turns into a lofty suffering; and was also capable in the sequences about Isaiah Berlin of mythologising ('There was no Romeo but there certainly was an Aeneas'), and in *Poem Without a Hero* of weaving a complex tapestry of emotions and unfulfilled expectations. She was also capable of reacting to a woman in a prison queue's simple plea: 'Could you describe this?', and going on in a documentary form, never without allegory, to transform the horrors of reality into great art.

The judgement of the critic Kornei Chukovsky seems to intensify over the years. In 1921, in an essay in *Dom Iskusstv*, he wrote: 'From her first book it was obvious that she was the poet of the orphans, the widows; that her poetry was nourished on the feeling of not belonging, parting and loss.' In 1921 Nikolai Gumilyov had been shot, for alleged conspiracy in an anti-Bolshevik plot, although according to recent Soviet thinking, his "guilt" lay in his code of honour that did not allow him to reveal his knowledge of such a plot's existence. In the 30s her third husband N. Punin had been arrested (described in *Requiem*, I) and her son Lev Gumilyov was first arrested. He was also in and out of labour camp until 1956. Nadezhda Mandelstam thought that he was in effect being held hostage by the authorities in order to exert pressure on his mother.

Anna Akhmatova, who died on 5 March 1966, outlived her

three fellow-poets and contemporaries Osip Mandelstam (died [?] 27 December 1938), Marina Tsvetayeva (died 31 August 1941) and Boris Pasternak (died 30 May 1960).

In *A Wreath for the Dead*, a cycle of poems written at various times to friends and writers of the epoch, Akhmatova writes in living memory of these people. Further, her relationship to Baudelaire, Verlaine, Nerval, Dante and Shakespeare and to many other writers, culminating with Pushkin, was a living one. Memory, reminiscence and memorialising become an integral part of the long *Poem Without a Hero.* Losev, the journalist and poet, has written recently (*Kontinent* no.55) on the search for the hero in *Poem Without a Hero*. Although there may be a case for finding the hero in the City of Petersburg/Leningrad, or in the Age/Time, I think the hero could equally be Mnemosyne, the muse of memory. I have included in this book some of the Note on the *Poem*, and indeed the Ballet Libretto of the *Poem*, in the hope that Akhmatova's words, and the comments of critics on the *Poem Without a Hero* will cast some light on this complex work. When I first translated Akhmatova 20 years ago for the *Selected Poems of Anna Akhmatova* (Penguin Books and Oxford University Press) I did not then approach the theme of The Guest from the Future, the Cycles to Isaiah Berlin or *Poem Without a Hero*, which Akhmatova worked on from 1940 to 1962. Joseph Brodsky, flying in the face of traditional thinking, has said in an interview in Russian in *Vremya i My* (no.97) that this long poem is 'easy to decode'. Speculation as to who is who in the poem (including three or four candidates for one of the roles in the masquerade) is relieved by the fact that as Isaiah Berlin has succinctly put it: 'some of the figures which occur in *Poem Without a Hero*...may represent the fusion of two or more persons, real imaginary or symbolic'. Nadezhda Mandelstam, Akhmatova's friend and an acute and sympathetic critic, has mentioned how offensive she found Akhmatova's use of doubles in the case of the young dragoon Vsevolod Knyazyev, who committed suicide, and Osip Mandelstam, who survived only to die in his 40s on his way to a labour camp in eastern Siberia.

If Akhmatova is settling old scores in *Poem Without a Hero*, she seems to pay for them by assuming an enormous burden of guilt, a theme that comes up time and time again in her poetry, for instance in *Fragments of Pottery* (p.124):

> I am the most guilty person on earth –
> in the past, in the present and in the future.

Out of this isolating personal and national suffering and the solitude and steadfastness that she needed in order to write her poems she erected a monument which will last longer than any edifice. But to say it is a monument is in many senses wrong. It is monumental but not monolithic, for it is made up of memorable fragments – of poetry – carried in the hearts and minds of millions of Russians. Respect for the Word was an Acmeist tenet. Indeed, Nikolai Gumilyov had written in his poem 'The Word': 'and in the Gospel according to St John it is written that the word is God'. It is to Language, which is not so much inherited as handed on, and, of course specifically her own great Russian language, that Akhmatova is speaking in the Churchillian poem 'Courage' (p.150).

The dignity and solemnity of Akhmatova's poetry is legendary but there are also delicious touches of irony, sarcasm, satire and allegory. Her poetry can cross from culture to culture, from language to language. To Russians she is Conscience, Craft and Memory. To us in the West she is more than a great woman poet, she is a representative of the highest human spirit. We are all the heirs of Akhmatova.

RICHARD McKANE
London, 1989

Translator's Note and Acknowledgements

Russian Texts of Anna Akhmatova

In general I have used the excellent three volume *Collected Works* of Anna Akhmatova, edited by Struve and Filippov (1963–83: volumes I and II, Inter-Language Literary Associates, West Germany; volume III, YMCA, Paris). The extensive revisions to this collection, some of which corrected serious errors and omissions pointed out by Akhmatova herself (who saw volume I before she died) make it the best text to work from, although I do not agree with the inclusion of the Cycle *Glory to Peace* in volume II, which Akhmatova wrote in an attempt to get her son Lev Gumilyov out of labour camp. I have also used the Soviet Biblioteka Poeta Edition (1976), edited by Academician V. Zhirmunsky, and the recent Soviet Edition (1987) edited by M. Dudin.

However, I have departed from all three editions in introducing, in chronological order, some poems not included in *The Flight of Time*, Akhmatova's last book, published in 1965. A "canon" of Akhmatova's work does not exist, and I felt it important to put the poems that were outside the statutory seven "books" into these books, as I believe Akhmatova would have wished. These poems are marked with an asterisk in the Contents, and will be found in the Russian either in volume III of Struve/Filippov, or (for Zhirmunsky and Dudin had already started this process) chronologically or at the end of the *Seventh Book* in the Soviet Editions.

With the publication of *Requiem* in the journals *Neva* and *Oktyabr* in the Soviet Union (1987) a new era is starting in the publication of Akhmatova, including the publication by Lydia Chukovskaya of *Fragments of Pottery* in the magazine *Gorizont*. Indeed, this edition includes a number of poems first published since 1973, when the Soviet Union became a signatory to the Berne Convention on copyright; their inclusion has been authorised by the official Soviet literary agency VAAP.

On the Translation

I would encourage English readers to turn to the Russian of Anna

Akhmatova with the assistance of these translations. In the original they will find precise, elegant, rhyming structures, and a rich Russian: robust, yet full of tenderness, *toska* (anguish), and poignancy, yet purposeful and – certainly in *Poem Without a Hero* – with a driving and inexorable rhythm of language and thought that used to overwhelm her.

I decided, even in the Penguin *Selected Poems of Anna Akhmatova* (1969) to follow the rhythm of image, metaphor and vocabulary, rather than rhyme and metre.

This book is an almost complete later poems, with a representative selection of early poems. Akhmatova's own titles of the poems are printed without inverted commas. I have used first lines or half first lines as "contingency titles" where, as is frequently the case in Russian poetry, there are no titles.

Acknowledgements

My friend Peter Levi, alone of English poets, gave me the initial encouragement which set me on the road to translating poetry, especially Anna Akhmatova, and to my becoming a poet.

Many of my insights into Anna Akhmatova arose out of meetings with Amanda Haight in the late 60s. Her book, which includes translations of many poems, *Anna Akhmatova: A Poetic Pilgrimage* (Oxford University Press, 1976), revived these memories. All readers of Akhmatova are indebted to her, and her biography is still the best book on Akhmatova in any language. Amanda Haight made Akhmatova live for me and I thank her for it.

Sir Isaiah Berlin, who visited Akhmatova in Leningrad in 1945, saw her twenty years later in Oxford, when she received her Honorary Doctorate, and is such a central figure in her poetry and life, encouraged me greatly, illuminating his own role as he tells it in *Personal Impressions* (Oxford University Press).

The two volume *Memoirs of Anna Akhmatova* (YMCA in Russian) by Lydia Chukovskaya, and a new book on Akhmatova by Anatoly Naiman (shortly to be published in English) revealed to me aspects of Akhmatova's daily life as well her poetry. Very close to publication I was able to read Jessie Davies's useful book on Akhmatova, *Anna of All the Russias*.

A fundamental role in my reapproaching Akhmatova was played for me by Harvey Karmen, Esther Knox, Sue Reid and

Anthony Fry. William Shawcross and Robert Moxon-Browne gave me the kind of logistic support and faith I needed. Arthur Cooper, my late friend, translator from the Chinese, philologist and poet, shared with me his insights on language.

Ruth and James Christie read many of the translations, made useful suggestions, and tracked down an important James Joyce quotation. Alice Barstow combed the Russian and English with a fine precision. Tom Sinclair helped me with the prose passages, and Feyyaz Fergar with the *Seventh Book*. Helen Szamuely helped me revise *Requiem* and other Akhmatova poems for readings. Peter Norman generously shared with me his knowledge of Akhmatova. Sir Dimitri Obolensky gave me insights through our readings of Akhmatova together at the GB-USSR Association and Pushkin Club, where many of these poems came alive for me in English in Margaret Robertson's voice.

Several Russian friends in London, and one in particular, gave me advice which made me radically develop my thinking on Akhmatova and led me to make considerable improvements to the translations, and I was aware throughout the late 60s, 70s and 80s as I worked on this book that I was acknowledging a debt not only to Marlborough College and Oxford University, where I had learned Russian, but also a massive but anonymous one to Russia itself, and my understanding of her. Times and attitudes have changed: the vast majority of Anna Akhmatova's work has been published in the Soviet Union; a case can even be made out for Akhmatova being a *glasnost* writer.

In 1978 I was awarded the Hodder Fellowship in the Humanities at Princeton University. This put me into contact with two other writers who have worked on Akhmatova, Stephen Berg, the poet and editor of *American Poetry Review*, and the poet Stanley Kunitz. Stephen Berg introduced me to Elizabeth McKane, to whom this book is dedicated. She helped me enormously with the intricacies of the English poems at a stage, familiar to other translators, when I could move the poems no further on my own. Working on a poet you love with someone you love is a deep and moving experience. It is also for our little daughter Juliet, who prefers poems and translations to be read not in 'a poetry voice' that this book is written.

Selected Poems

ANNA AKHMATOVA, 1917

Briefly About Myself

I was born on 11 (23) June 1889 at Bolshoi Fontan near Odessa. My father was then a retired Naval Engineer. When I was one year old we moved to the North to live in Tsarskoye Selo. I lived there till I was sixteen.

My first memories are of Tsarskoye Selo: the damp, green grandeur of the parks, the common where my nanny used to take me, the hippodrome where the piebald ponies galloped, the old railway station and other things that went into 'Tsarskoye Selo Ode' [p.223].

I spent every summer near Sebastopol at the Streletskaya Bay, and there I made friends with the sea. The old Chersonese near where we lived was the strongest impression of those years.

I learnt to read from Leo Tolstoy's collection of children's stories. At the age of five, listening to the governess with the older children, I also began to speak French.

I wrote my first poem at the age of eleven. For me poetry began with Pushkin, Lermontov and Derzhavin ('To the Purple Mantle Born') and Nekrasov ('Frost, Red-Nose'). My mother knew these poems by heart.

I went to school at the Tsarskoye Selo Girls' Gymnasium. At first school went badly, then a lot better – but I was always a reluctant student.

In 1905 my parents parted and Mama and the children went to the South. We lived for a whole year in Yevpatoria where I did the penultimate year of the Gymnasium at home, pined for Tsarskoye Selo and wrote a mass of hopeless poetry. The reverberations of the 1905 revolution scarcely reached isolated Yevpatoria. I studied my last year of school at the Fundukleyev Gymnasium in Kiev and finished in 1907.

I entered the Law Faculty of the Higher Women's Academy in Kiev. I was happy studying history of law and especially Latin, but I lost interest in the courses when they became purely legal.

In 1910 (25 April Old Style) I married N.S. Gumilyov and we went to Paris for a month.

The laying out of the boulevards on the living body of Paris (which Zola described) was not quite complete (Boulevard Raspail). Werner, Edison's friend, showed me two tables in the Taverne de Panthéon and said: 'Here are your social democrats: these are the Bolsheviks, and those are the Mensheviks.' Women, with varying degrees of success, wore trousers (jupes culottes), or swathed their legs (jupes entravées). Poetry was in the wilderness – people bought it just because of the illustrations by more or less famous artists. I realised then that Parisian art had swallowed up French poetry.

After moving to Petersburg I joined Rayev's History and Literature Courses. I was already writing the poems which were to go into my first book.

When I saw a proof copy of Innokenty Annensky's *Cypress Chest* I was stunned and was oblivious of everything as I read it.

The crisis of Symbolism came about in 1910, and poets who were starting out no longer joined that movement. Some went to Futurism, others to Acmeism. Together with my First Poets' Guild comrades – Mandelstam, Zenkevich, and Narbut – I became an Acmeist.

I spent the spring of 1911 in Paris, where I witnessed the first triumphs of the Russian ballet. In 1912 I travelled in Northern Italy (Genoa, Pisa, Bologna, Padua, Venice). Italian painting and architecture made a huge impression on me, like a dream that one remembers all one's life.

In 1912 my first book of poetry *Evening* came out, in only 300 copies. The critics were favourable.

My only son was born on 1 October 1912.

In March 1914 my second book, *Rosary*, came out. Its life span was about six weeks – the Petersburg season started to die at the beginning of May. Everyone went off somewhere. This time the parting with Petersburg was to be forever. We returned not to Petersburg but to Petrograd, from the XIXth century straight into the XXth. Everything changed, starting with the look of the city. It would seem that a little book of love lyrics of a author, who was starting out, would be drowned in world events. Time decided otherwise.

I spent every summer in old Tver Province, twenty miles or so from Bezhetsk. It was not a picturesque place: fields ploughed in neat squares on the hills, mills, quagmires, dried-up marshes, gates, and cornfields everywhere. There I wrote many of the poems that went into *Rosary* and *White Flock*. *White Flock* came out in September 1917.

Readers and critics have been unjust in regard to this book. For some reason they consider that it was less successful than *Rosary*. This collection appeared under even more menacing circumstances. There was no transport – the book couldn't even be sent to

Moscow – it sold out in Petrograd alone. The journals were closing down, and the newspapers too. So, unlike *Rosary*, *White Flock* had no publicity. The hunger and the havoc grew daily. I find it strange that these circumstances are not taken into consideration.

I worked in the Agricultural Institute Library after the October Revolution. My book of poems *Wayside Grass* came out in 1921, and in 1922 the book *Anno Domini*.

From about the mid-Twenties I became engrossed in research into the architecture of Petersburg and the life and art of Pushkin. The fruits of my Pushkin studies were three works – on the 'Golden Cockerel', on 'Adolfe' of Benjamin Constant, and on 'The Stone Guest'. In time they were all published.

The works 'Alexandrine', 'Pushkin and the Neva Estuary' and 'Pushkin in 1828', which I have been working on for the last twenty years, will, presumably, be included in a book called *The Death of Pushkin*.

From the mid-Twenties my new poems virtually stopped being published nor were my old ones republished.

The Patriotic War of 1941 found me in Leningrad. At the end of September, after the blockade had started, I flew out to Moscow.

I lived in Tashkent up till May 1944, hungering for news of Leningrad and the front. Like other poets I often read my poems to the wounded soldiers in the hospitals. It was in Tashkent that I first learned the meaning of the shade of trees and the sound of water in the scorching heat. I also learned the meaning of human kindness: I was often seriously ill in Tashkent.

In May 1944 I flew in to the Moscow spring, full of joyful hopes and looking forward to the coming victory. I returned to Leningrad in June.

The terrifying apparition, which pretended to be my city, so struck me that I recorded my meeting with it in prose. The essays 'Three Lilacs' and 'Visiting Death' – the last about a poetry reading at the front at Teriok – were written then. Prose has always been both a secret and a temptation for me. From the very beginning I knew all there was to know about poetry, but I never knew anything about prose. Everybody praised my first experiment to the skies, but I did not trust them. I called Zoshchenko. He ordered me to take out some parts but said that he agreed with the rest. I was happy. But then after the arrest of my son I burnt it along with the whole of my archive.

The question of literary translation has interested me for many years. I did a lot of translations in the post-war years. I am still translating.

In 1962 I finished *Poem Without a Hero* which I had been writing for 22 years.

Last winter, just before the Dante anniversary celebrations, I heard the Italian language again. I spent some time in Rome and Sicily. In the spring of 1965 I went to Shakespeare's homeland, saw the British sky and the Atlantic, met old friends and new ones, and visited Paris again.

I have never stopped writing poems. For me they are my connection with time, with the new life of my people. In writing them I was living in the rhythms which were to be heard in the heroic history of my country. I am happy that I have lived in these times and seen events, the like of which have never been.

From Fragments from Memoirs

The Beginning

I was born in 1889 the same year, as Charlie Chaplin and Tolstoy's *Kreutzer Sonata*, (H)itler, the Eiffel Tower, and, it seems, Eliot. That summer Paris was celebrating the hundredth anniversary of the storming of the Bastille. On the night of my birth – Ivanov's Night, 23 June, the ancient Midsummer Night celebrations are held.

I was named Anna in honour of my grandmother Anna Yegorovna Motovilova. Her mother was the Tatar princess Akhmatova, descended from Genghis Khan, whose name I made my *nom de plume*, not imagining that I was going to become a Russian poet. I was born in the Sarakini *dacha* (Bolshoi Fontan, 11th stop on the railway) near Odessa. This little dacha (or rather hut) stood at the bottom of a narrow strip of land which led sharply down, alongside the post office. The sea shore is very steep there and the tracks went right along the edge.

When I was fifteen and we were living in a *dacha* in Lustdorf, we were somehow passing by this place and Mama suggested that I drop in and look at the Sarakini *dacha*, which I had not seen since. At the entrance to the hut I said: 'There will be a memorial plaque here one day.' I was not being vain. It was just a stupid joke. Mama got upset and said: 'My God, I have brought you up badly.'

Certainly the 9th of January and Tsushima [the disastrous defeat and sinking of the Russian fleet by the Japanese in 1905. Tr.] was a shock that reverberated my whole life through, and since it was the first, it was especially terrifying. 1910 was the year of the crisis of Symbolism, the deaths of Leo Tolstoy and Komissarzhevskaya [leader of an actors' troupe attached to Meyerhold. Tr.]. 1911 was the year of the Chinese Revolution, which changed the face of Asia, and the year of the diaries of Blok, full of foreboding.

The XXth century started in autumn 1914, together with the war, in the same way as the XIXth century started with the Vienna Congress. There is no doubt that Symbolism was a 19th century phenomenon. Our rebellion against Symbolism was perfectly reasonable, because we felt ourselves to be twentieth century people and we did not want to remain in the past...

These poor poems of a most empty girl have for some reason been reprinted thirteen times...That girl herself (as far as I remember) did not foresee such a fate for them and hid the journals in which they had been printed under the cushions of the sofa: 'So as not to get upset!' And she was so upset that *Evening* had appeared that she went off to Italy (spring 1912) and sitting in the tram she looked at the other passengers and thought: how lucky they are not to have a book out.

Petersburg

When I went to the Sestroretsk resort with Nikolai Nikolaevich (Gumilyov), we always returned through Beloostrov. The railway line went most of the time through a dense, dark conifer forest. The Germans, I mean the Finns, burnt down these woods. Now there are only stumps and occasional bushes. So many events since then! Every time I go into town from Komarovo I remember all this.

After Petersburg as I found it (at that time I was, in the full sense of the word, only an observer), I will say a few words about Petersburg of the 1910s, about wartime Petersburg, and about revolutionary Petrograd. About the unforgettable year 1919 (for some reason completely forgotten) and, finally about Leningrad after the blockade. So many layers! These themes are touched in on in some way in my *Poem Without a Hero*, and I described Leningrad after the blockade in detail after my return from Tashkent, to which I was evacuated.

The two windows in the Mikhailovskoye castle remained the same as in 1801, and it seemed that behind them they were still killing Paul; and the Semyonov barracks and the Semyonov parade ground, where Dostoyevsky waited to be executed, and Fountain House – a whole symphony of horrors...The Sheremetev limes, the house-spirits calling to each other...the Summer Garden...The first – fragrant, fallen quiet in the July stillness, and the second – underwater in 1924. The Summer Garden again, cut up into foul-smelling trenches in 1941, and the Field of Mars, where they drilled the conscripts in 1915 (drum roll) and the Field of Mars – a pockmarked back garden, half-abandoned (1921) under a cloud of crows' wings, and the gates through which the members of 'People's Will' [terrorist wing of the populist movement who assassinated Alexander II in 1881. Tr.] were led out to be executed.

Petersburg yard noises. First, the firewood being thrown through the cellar window. The organ-grinders: ('Sing, my swallow, sing, and calm my heart!...') The knife-grinders: ('I sharpen knives, scissors!!!') The old-clothes dealers ('Dresses and clothes!') who were always Tatars. The tinsmiths: ('I've got Vyborg pretzels'). The noise of the bucket scraping on the well in the yards.

Recently I heard someone say 'The 1910s were the most tasteless time'; that's what one is meant to say nowadays, I suppose; but still I answered: apart from anything else this was the time of Stravinsky and Blok, Anna Pavlova and Skryabin, Rostovtsev and Chaliapin, Meyerhold and Diaghilev.

Slepnyovo

Once I was in Slepnyovo in winter. It was grand. Everything moved back into the XIXth century, almost into Pushkin's time. Sleighs, boots, fur travelling rugs, huge, short fur coats, ringing silence, snowdrifts, diamond snows. Back in Petersburg, Rasputin had already been killed and people were waiting for the Revolution...

Slepnyovo for me is like an arch is for architecture...at first small, then larger and larger and finally – total freedom, so to speak.

The smells of the Pavlovsk station. I am fated to remember them all my life as though I were deaf, dumb and blind. The first – smoke from the antediluvian steam train which carried me to the Tyalev Park, the *salon de music* (which they used to call the *'solyony muzhik'* ['salty peasant'. Tr.], the second – the worn parquet floor, then the smell from the hairdressers, third – strawberries, Pavlovsk ones, from the station shop, fourth – mignonette and roses (cool in the blazing heat), fresh moist buds which are on sale in the flower kiosk (on the left), then cigars and the rich restaurant food. And the ghost of Nastasia Filippovna [from Dostoyevsky's *The Idiot*. Tr.]. Tsarskoye was always on weekdays because it was *chez nous*, Pavlovsk on weekends and holidays because we had to go somewhere and because it was far from home...

About Annensky

Whereas Balmont and Bryusov themselves completed what they
had begun (although they confused the provincial graphomaniacs
for a long time), Annensky's *cause* came alive with a terrible force
in the next generation. If he had not died so early he would have
been able to see his thunder showers lashing the pages of B.
Pasternak, his semi-futurist and surreal 'Dedu Lidu ladili' in
Khlebnikov, his street theatre (balloons) in Mayakovsky etc.
However I do not want to say that everyone imitated him. But he
went down so many roads at the same time. He carried with him
so many new things that all the innovators were his kin. I talked
with Pasternak in the autumn of 1935. Boris Leonidovich grasped
this theme with characteristic eloquence and asserted categorical-
ly that Annensky had played a significant role in his art...I talked
with Osip (Mandelstam) about Annensky several times. He too
always spoke about Annensky with a faithful reverence. I don't
know if M. Tsvetayeva knew Annensky. There is a love and
worship of the Master in the poems and prose of Gumilyov.

About Blok

I consider Blok to be not only the greatest European poet of the
first quarter of the twentieth century (I mourned bitterly his
premature death), but also the man of the epoch – i.e. the most
characteristic representative of the time...but I knew him very
little. At the time when we met (about ten times) I was not
concerned with him and when that gossip, of presumably provin-
cial origin, reached me I just laughed. Now, however, when it
threatens to distort my poems and even my biography, I do
consider it necessary to dwell on this question. I regret deeply that
my three letters to Blok (in answer to his well-known letters that
have been printed) have evidently been lost. All that I remember
about Blok could be put on one ordinary-sized page, and the only
interesting thing is his remark about Leo Tolstoy...

About O. Mandelstam

Above all I do not want to create a 'respectable' biography for Mandelstam. He does not need it anyway. This was a man with the soul of a down-and-out in the highest sense of the term and a *poète maudit par excellence*, as his biography proved. He was always being attracted to the South, the sea, new places. The 1929 cycle of immortal poems bear witness to his frenzied love affair with Armenia.

15 February 1960...One could not praise anyone in front of Osip – he would get angry and argue and be unbelievably unjust, arrogant and cutting. But if anyone criticised the same person in front of him, the same thing would happen and he would defend him with all his might.

As for the grasshopper-clock singing – that was us lighting the stove; I had a fever – I was taking my temperature and the fever was rustling, ('And the dry stove rustles'), that was the red silk burning.

'Sometimes I get the impression of flight from your poems. Today I didn't get this, but it has to be. Make sure that it is always there. These lines of yours can only be extracted from my brain by a surgical procedure.' (about something in *Rosary*). On the subject of some poems by N. Bruni he went into a frenzy and growled: 'There are poems which I take as a personal insult.' Note and attempt to explain the different relations of Moscow and Leningrad to Mandelstam (30s)...In 1920 Mandelstam saw Petersburg as half-Venice, and half-theatre.

Gumilyov and Africa

Tent is a made-to-order geography book in verse and bears no relationship to his travels. He was in Cairo in 1908 (Ezbekie). There were two journeys. One lasted 6 months. He went in autumn 1910 and returned on 25 March Old Style. He was in Addis Ababa, via Djibouti, in 1911. The second time he went in 1913 with *carte blanche* from the Academy of Sciences, with his nephew Nikolai Leonidovich Sverchkov (his sister's son) to seek out ethnographical objects. 'Shark Catching' (Article in *Noon*). There was an African Diary. In *Worlds and Days*, and in *Niva* ('Somali') there may be some details. Hunting in Africa (Narbut in Abyssinia). African fever. He gave a Triptych to Professor

Turayev. Recorded songs. N.B. Letters exist from his trips and the places he stayed in...Sverchkov's book about the 1913 travels was handed in to the publishers Grzhebin and evidently was lost there.

Makovsky believed the fable, which did not exist in the 1910s, and instead of writing about Gumilyov's participation in *Apollo*, about the origins of Acmeism, about the role of 'The Tower', he – an old man – covers himself with shame, passing on malodorous and utterly false tales of family life.

The fact that the 83 year old Makovsky, who has forgotten everything and muddled it all up, can rehash this cruel rubbish gives rise to nothing but pity. His evidence is so great isn't it! And all this is revenge on Akhmatova for not becoming an emigré. The second fable has more criminal intent. Someone wanted to misrepresent the image of the poet. We will not ponder the filthy reasons for his carrying this out, but my conscience does not allow me to leave this matter as it stands.

About Pasternak

Second Birth concludes the first period of lyrics. It's evident that there was no way out...A long and tormenting period followed (10 years) when he was actually unable to write a single line. I can see that before my eyes, and I hear his worried voice: 'What's happening to me?' A *dacha* appeared (Peredelkino) at first a summer one, then a winter one. Essentially he left the city for ever. There in the Moscow suburbs came the meeting with '*Nature*'. Nature, his whole life through, was his only fully-empowered Muse, his secret companion with whom he'd converse, his Fiancée and Belovèd, his Wife and Widow – Nature was to him what Russia was to Blok. He stayed faithful to her to the end and she rewarded him royally. In June 1941, when I arrived in Moscow he told me on the telephone: 'I've written 9 poems. I'll come and read them,' and he came over. He said 'This is only the beginning. I am in the witness stand.' I now realise that the most terrible thing about Pasternak was that he never "remembers" anything. In the whole cycle *When It Clears Up*, when he is an old man really, he never "remembers" anything: neither his dear ones, his love or his youth...

We don't make of it a soul
object for sale and barter,
and we being sick, poverty-stricken, unable to utter a word,
don't even remember about it.
                    (p. 225)

About M. Tsvetayeva

Our first and last two-day meeting occurred in June 1941 at
Bolshaya Ordynka, No.17, in the Ardovs' flat (the first day) and
in Marina Roshcha at Kharzhiev's (the second and final day). It is
terrible to think how Marina herself would have described these
meetings if *she* had remained alive and *I* had died on 31 August
1941. It would have been a "fragrant legend" as our grandfathers
used to say. Perhaps it would be a lament of a twenty-five year
love which turned out in vain, but in all events it would have been
grand. Now when she has returned to her Moscow, a queen for
always...I want to remember those *Two Days* simply and
"without legend".

About Vyacheslav Ivanov

Vyacheslav Ivanov was not the attractor and seducer of us, the
youth of that time. In the emigration Vyacheslav Ivanov began to
think of himself as Vyacheslav the Grand of the Tower. There was
no grandeur at Tavricheskaya. But evidently in emigration the
same psychology appeared as in wartime evacuation, when
everyone thought that they had come from palaces and stately
homes.

About Poetry

If it is fate that Poetry will flourish in the 20th century in my
homeland in particular, I make bold to say that I have always
been a joyful and trustworthy witness...And I am certain that we
still do not know to the full what a magical chorus of poets we are
endowed with and that the Russian language is young and
flexible and that we are writing fresh poems and that we love
them and believe in them.

A Fleeting Biography

I.

The winters were in Tsarskoye. Summers (the Tara *dacha*) were in the Crimea, but it is impossible to convince anyone of this because they think I am Ukrainian. Firstly because of my father's name – Gorenko – and secondly because I was born in Odessa (and graduated from the Fundukleyevsky Gymnasium...)

In fact I lived longer in Tashkent (in evacuation from 1941 to 1944) than in Kiev, where I spent one winter at the Fundukleyevsky Gymnasium and two winters at the Higher Women's College. But the inattentiveness of people to one another knows no limits. The reader of this book must get used to the fact that nothing was like that, then and there, as it seems to him. It's a terrible thing to say but people only see what they want to see and hear only what they want to hear. Basically they talk to themselves, without listening to the person they are talking with. 90% of the monstrous rumours, false reputations, and sacredly treasured gossip are based on this characteristic of human nature. (To this day we preserve the serpent's hiss of Poletika about Pushkin!!!) I ask those who do not agree with me to remember what they have heard about themselves.

II.

As far as the eye could see no one in the family wrote poetry, but the first Russian poetess Anna Bunina was the aunt of my grandfather, Erasmus Ivanovich Stogov. The Stogovs were landowners of modest means of the Mozhayevsky district of the Moscow province, resettled there after the revolt during Governor Martha's time. In Novgorod they were wealthier and more distinguished.

A hired Russian murderer killed my ancestor Khan Ahmat in his tent at night, and Karamzin relates that the Mongol yoke was finished at this stroke. On this date, to mark the happy event, there used to be a religious procession from the Sretensk monastery in Moscow. This Ahmat, as is well known, was descended from Genghis Khan. One of these Akhmatov princesses – Praskovya Yegorovna, got married in the XVIIth century to a rich and distinguished landowner Motovilov. Yegor Motovilov was my great-grandfather and his daughter, Anna Yegorovna was my grandmother. She died when my mother was 9 years old, and I was named Anna in her honour. Several rings, set with diamonds and one with an emerald, were made from her tiara, but I couldn't wear her own ring, even though my fingers were slender.

The Wild Girl

Pagan childhood. The folk in the area round the Otrada *dacha* (the Streletskaya Bay, the Chersonese) gave me the nickname of the Wild Girl, because I used to walk around barefoot and hatless etc. and jumped into the open sea off the boat, bathed in the stormy sea, and got so burned that I peeled: all this shocked the provincial Sebastopol ladies.

*   *   *

My childhood was just as unique and grand as the childhood of children the world over...

It is both easy and difficult to talk about childhood. Because of its stasis it's easy to describe it, but too often a sugariness filters into this description, which is completely alien to such an important and deep period of life. Apart from this, some people want to make out their childhood was too unhappy, and others too happy. Usually both of these versions are rubbish. Children have nothing to make comparisons with, and they simply don't know if they are happy or not. Immediately consciousness appears, man falls into a completely ready and immovable world, and the most natural thing is not to believe that this world could have been other than what it was. This primordial picture remains in the soul of man, and people do exist who believe only in it, somehow concealing the strangeness of this. Conversely, others do not believe at all in the reality of this picture and repeat, similarly absurdly: 'Was that really me?'

Somewhere round about the age of 50 the beginning of life returns to one. This explains some of my poems of 1940 ('Willow' [p.132], 'My young hand' [p.173]) which, as is well known, gave rise to the criticism that I was drawn back into the past.

*   *   *

...In 1936 I started writing again, but my handwriting had changed, and my voice sounded different. Life was leading by the bridle a Pegasus that reminded one of the pale horses of the Apocalypse, or the black horse of those poems that had not been born then...There could be no return to the first style. I am not the one to judge whether this was for the better or for the worse. 1940 was the apogee. The poems were constantly making themselves heard, treading on each others' heels, in haste and out of breath, and sometimes, probably – bad.

*   *   *

Anna's room looked out on the Bezymyanny ['Anonymous.' Tr.] side-street, which was covered in winter with snowdrifts, and overgrown in summer with weeds, luxurious nettles and giant burdocks...There was a bed, a little table to do homework on, and a bookshelf. There was a candle in a brass candlestick (there being no electricity yet). There was an ikon in the corner. No effort had been made to decorate the stern surroundings, either with knick-knacks, hangings or cards.

In Tsarskoye Selo she did everything that a well brought up young lady should do. She knew how to fold her arms as she should, to curtsey, to answer politely and briefly in French the questions of an old lady. She fasted in Holy Week in the Gymnasium church. Occasionally her father took her to the opera (still in her school uniform), to the Mariinsky Theatre where they sat in a box. She used to go to the Hermitage, the Museum of Alexander III. In spring and summer she went to Pavlovsk and the music in the Station. She went to the Museums and the Exhibitions of Painting...In winter she often went skating in the park.

There was a feeling of antiqueness about the Tsarskoye Selo parks also, but it was completely different (the statues). She read all the time. I think that the biggest influence on her was the then Lord of Thoughts Knut Hamsun (*Enigmas and the Secret*); *Pan* certainly and *Victoria* to a lesser extent. The other powerful influence was Ibsen...

* The Memoirs in the third person, and some other passages, were written by V. Sreznevskaya, Akhmatova's lifelong friend, working in close collaboration with Akhmatova.

EVENING

'The pillow'

The pillow is already
hot on both sides.
Now the second candle
goes out and the crows' calls
become louder.
I haven't slept tonight.
It's too late to think of sleep.
How unbearably white
is the shutter on the white window.
             Good morning!

'I couldn't get to sleep'

I couldn't get to sleep all night –
they were talking anxiously in loud voices.
Someone was going on a long journey
and taking the sick child,
and mother wrung her withered
hands in the ill-lit hall
and searched in the dark
for the clean little bonnet
and the baby-blanket.

[Kiev, 1909]

The Grey-Eyed King

Glory to you unrelenting pain!
Yesterday the grey-eyed king died.

The autumn night was stifling and crimson,
my husband on returning said calmly:

'You know they carried him from the hunt,
they found the body by the old oak.

Poor queen. He was so young!
In one night she turned grey.'

He found his pipe on the fireplace
and went off to his night work.

I will wake my little daughter now,
and look into her little grey eyes.

Outside the window the poplars rustle:
'Your king is on this earth no more.'

[1910]

Love

Now coiled like a tiny snake
it casts spells by the very heart,
now for whole days like a little dove
it coos by the window,

now it sparkles in bright hoarfrost,
is glimpsed in the somnolence of wallflowers...
but truly and secretly it leads away
from joy and from peace.

It knows how to sob so sweetly
in the prayer of an aching violin,
and it's terrifying to divine it
in a still unfamiliar smile.

[Tsarskoye Selo, 1911]

'The boy who plays the bagpipes'

The boy who plays the bagpipes,
the girl who weaves her wreath,
two paths crossed in the forest,
a small distant fire within a distant field.

I see everything, I retain everything,
lovingly, tenderly I cherish it in my heart.
The one man I never knew
I cannot remember any more.

I do not ask for wisdom or strength,
no, just let me warm myself by the fire!
I feel cold...Neither winged nor wingless,
no joyful god visits me.

[1911]

'In the memory the sun grows dimmer'

In the memory the sun grows dimmer,
the grass is turning brown,
the wind flutters the early snowflakes
gently, gently.

The water freezes. The narrow canals
do not flow,
nothing will ever happen here,
ever!

In the empty sky the willow spread
a transparent fan.
Perhaps it's better that I did not become
your wife.

In the memory the sun grows dimmer.
What is this? Darkness?
Perhaps! Within a night it will be
winter.

[1911]

'The door is half open'

The door is half open,
the lime trees wave sweetly...
On the table, forgotten –
a whip and a glove.

The lamp casts a yellow circle...
I listen to the rustling.
Why did you go?
I don't understand...

Tomorrow the morning
will be clear and happy.
This life is beautiful,
heart, be wise;

you are utterly tired,
you beat calmer, duller...
You know, I read
that souls are immortal.

[Tsarskoye Selo, 1911]

Song of the Last Meeting

My heart was helplessly cold,
but my steps were light.
I put my left glove
on my right hand.

It seemed there were many steps,
but I knew there were only three.
Autumn whispered among
the maples: 'Will you die with me!

I am deceived by my changing, wicked,
melancholy fate.'
I answered: 'My darling, my darling!
I too – I'll die with you...'

This is the song of the last meeting.
I looked at the dark house:
only in the bedroom the candles burning
with a dispassionate yellow flame.

[Tsarskoye Selo, 1911]

'You suck my soul'

You suck my soul through a straw.
I know it tastes bitter and intoxicating.
But I will not beg you to stop the torture.
For many weeks this has been my peaceful chamber.

Say when you're through. It is not sad
that my soul is not in this world.
I'll take the short road
to see the children playing.

The gooseberry bushes are in flower.
Beyond the fence they're carrying bricks.
Who are you: my brother or my lover?
I don't remember and do not need to.

How bright it is here, but homeless
the tired body rests.
The passers-by seem to be thinking:
she must be a recent widow.

[Tsarskoye Selo, 1911]

In the Forest

Four diamonds — four eyes —
two of the owl and two of mine.
The end of this terrible tale
is how my bridegroom died.

I lie on the thick, moist grass,
my words ring senselessly,
looking down self-importantly
the owl listens keenly to them.

Fir trees crowd close round us,
over us the sky – a black square;
you know, you know they killed him,
my elder brother killed him –

not in a bloody duel,
not on the battlefield, not in war,
but on the deserted forest path,
when he, in love, was coming to me.

[1911]

'I live like a cuckoo in a clock'

I live like a cuckoo in a clock.
I don't envy the birds in the woods.
They wind me – and I cuckoo.
I could only wish
this fate
on an enemy.

[1911]

'He loved three things'

He loved three things in this world:
evensong, white peacocks,
and faded maps of America.
He didn't like crying children,
he didn't like raspberry jam with his tea –
and womanish hysterics.
...And I was his wife.

[1911]

'Today they brought no letter'

Today they brought no letter for me:
he forgot to write or maybe he went away;
spring like a trill of silver laughter,
the boats are bobbing in the bay.
Today they brought no letter for me...

He was with me such a short time ago,
so in love, tender, mine,
but that was in white winter,
now it's spring, and spring's melancholy is poison.
He was with me such a short time ago.

I hear: a light, trembling fiddle-bow
is beating, beating in agony before death,
and I fear my heart will burst.
I will not finish these tender lines...

[1911]

Garden

The whole icebound garden
sparkles and crackles.
He who leaves me is sad,
but there is no path back.

The sun is just a round window,
a pale dull face, whose double
I secretly know, has pressed
against it for so long.

My calm is for ever taken up
with a premonition of trouble,
yesterday's footprints
still show through thin ice.

The dull, dead face looked down
over the dumb dream of the fields,
sharp cries of the last
migrating cranes fade.

White Night

Oh, I didn't lock the door,
didn't light the candles.
You don't know how tired I was
yet I decided not to go to bed.

I looked at the dying strip
of sunset in the dark firs,
drunk with the sound of a voice
just like yours.

To know that all is lost,
that life is complete hell!
Oh I was so certain
that you would come back.

[Tsarskoye Selo, 1911]

58

ROSARY

To M. Lozinsky

It drags on without end, this heavy amber day.
Impossible the sadness, vain the waiting!
Once more the deer speaks of the Northern Lights —
its silvered voice sounds in the deer park.
I believed that there was cool snow,
and a blue font for the sick and needy,
and a jolting ride on a small sledge
to the ancient chimes of distant bells.

[1912]

'I taught myself to live simply'

I taught myself to live simply and wisely,
to look at the sky and pray to God,
and to wander long before evening
to tire my superfluous worries.

When the burdocks rustle in the ravine
and the yellow-red rowanberry cluster droops
I compose happy verses
about life's decay, decay and beauty.

I come back. The fluffy cat
licks my palm, purrs so sweetly,
and the fire flares bright
on the saw-mill turret by the lake.

Only the cry of a stork landing on the roof
occasionally breaks the silence.
If you knock on my door
I may not even hear.

[1912]

Sleeplessness

Somewhere the cats are complaining and miaowing.
I catch the distant sounds of footsteps.
Your words lullaby me well,
they haven't let me sleep for three months.

You're with me, with me again sleeplessness!
I know your motionless face.
Come now my beauty, my illicit one,
don't you like my poem?

There are white curtains on the windows,
in the half-dark there is a stream of pale blue...
Have we taken comfort from the distant news?
Why is it all so easy with you?

[1912]

'I have come to replace you, sister'

'I have come to replace you, sister,
by the high forest bonfire.

Your hair has turned grey. Your eyes
have grown dim, the tears have misted them.

You no longer understand the birds' song,
you don't notice the stars or summer lightning.

You have not heard the sound of the tambourine for a long time
and I know silence terrifies you.

I have come to replace you, sister,
by the high forest bonfire.'

'You've come to bury me,
where are your spade and shovel?
You only hold a flute.
I'm not going to accuse you.
Is it not a pity that once long ago
my voice fell silent forever?

Put on my clothes,
forget my worries and alarm,
let the wind play in your hair.
You smell of lilac
and have come down a difficult path
to be radiant here.'

She went away on her own, giving up,
giving up her place to the other,
and made her way unsteadily like a blind woman
along a narrow unfamiliar path,

and she kept thinking that the flame
was near...that a hand held a tambourine...
She was like a white banner,
She was like the light from a beacon.

[1912]

In the Evening

There was such inexpressible sorrow
in the music in the garden.
The dish of oysters on ice
smelt fresh and sharp of the sea.

He said to me 'I am a true friend!'
He touched my dress.
There is no passion
in the touch of his hands.

This is how one strokes a cat or a bird,
this is how one looks at a shapely horsewoman.
There is only laughter in his eyes
under the light gold of his eyelashes.

The violins' mourning voices
sing above the spreading smoke:
'Give thanks to heaven:
you are alone with your love for the first time.'

[1913]

'We shall not drink from the same glass'

We shall not drink from the same glass
either water or wine.
We will not share early morning kisses,
or look out of the window at evening time.
You live by the sun and I live by the moon,
but one love is alive in us.

For me, my faithful, tender friend,
for you, your happy girl.
But I understand the fear in your grey eyes,
and you are guilty of causing my disease.
So short, so rare the meetings, and we'll keep it that way,
and so we're fated to preserve our peace.

Only your voice sings in my poems,
in your poems my soul wafts.
Oh there is a fire which neither oblivion
nor terror dare touch.
And if only you knew how I love
your dry, rose-pink lips right now.

[1913]

'I have a certain smile'

I have a certain smile.
A scarcely noticeable movement of the lips.
I keep it for you –
it is my gift of love.
I don't care that you're brash and vicious,
I don't care that you love others.
I am by the gilded lectern,
the grey-eyed bridegroom is with me.

[1913]

'Evening hours at the table'

Evening hours at the table.
An incorrigibly white page.
Mimosa smells of Nice and warm countries,
a big bird flies on a moonbeam.

I plait my hair tight at night
as though I will have need of my plaits tomorrow.
No longer sad, I look out of the window
at the sea and the sand dunes.

How much power has this man
who does not even ask for tenderness!
I cannot lift my tired eyelids
when he says my name.

'I know, I know, the skis'

I know, I know, the skis
will creak again drily.
A ginger moon in the blue sky,
the sweetly sloping meadow.

Distanced by silence,
the lights in the palace windows burn.
There is not a track, not a path,
and only the ice holes are dark.

Willow, tree of the water nymphs,
do not block my way!
In the snowy twigs black jackdaws,
black jackdaws shelter.

[Tsarskoye Selo, October 1913]

The Visitor

Everything as before: a fine snow
beats against the dining-room windows.
I have not changed,
though a man came to visit.

I asked: 'What do you want?'
He said 'To be with you in hell.'
I laughed, 'No doubt you'll
destroy us both.'

He lifted his thin hand
and softly touched the flowers:
'Tell me how they kiss you,
tell me how you kiss.'

He stared with resignation
at my wedding ring.
Not a single muscle moved
in his radiant, evil face.

I know: he delights in
knowing intensely and passionately,
that he needs nothing,
that I have nothing to refuse him.

[January 1914]

To Alexander Blok

I visited the poet.
Midday precisely, Sunday.
It was quiet in the spacious room.
There was frost outside the window,

and a crimson sun
above the shaggy, blue-grey smoke...
The silent host
looks at me so lucidly.

He has eyes which everyone
always remembers.
It is better for me to be careful
and not look into them at all.

But I remember a conversation,
a smoky midday, Sunday
in a tall, grey house
by the sea-gates of the Neva.

[1914]

WHITE FLOCK

'The blue varnish of the sky dims'

The blue varnish of the sky dims,
the song of the ocarina swells.
It is only a clay pipe,
no reason for it to complain like that.
Who told it my sins,
and why does it forgive me?...
Or does the voice recite me
your latest poems?

[1912]

'I will leave your white house'

I will leave your white house and quiet garden.
Life will be empty and bright.
I will glorify you, you in my poems,
as no woman can.
Remember your dear friend
in the heaven created by you for her eyes;
I trade in rarest goods —
I sell your love and tenderness.

'The fir wood is white'

The fir wood is white under the snow
through the patterned, smoky glass.
Why did you fly away without
saying goodbye, my clear-eyed hawk?

I listen to what people say,
and they say that you are a magician.
Since our meeting my old blue coat
feels tighter.

And the road to the country graveyard
has become a hundred times longer,
than when I simply used
to wander down it.

[1913]

'A black twisted road'

A black twisted road,
rain drizzled.
Someone asked if
he could take me home.
I agreed, but forgot
to look at him.
Later it was so strange
remembering that road.
The mist floated
like incense from a thousand censers.
My companion's insistent song
irritated my soul.
I remember the ancient gates
and the end of the road,
and there the man who walked with me
whispered: 'Farewell...'
He put a bronze crucifix in my hands,
as though he were my dear brother.
Wherever I go I hear
the song of the steppe.
I am at home, and not at home.
I cry and am sad...
Answer me, my stranger,
I am looking for you.

[1913]

'I see, I see the crescent moon'

I see, I see the crescent moon
through the willow's thick foliage.
I hear, I hear the regular beat
of unshod hooves.

You don't want to sleep either?
In a year you weren't able to forget me,
you're not used to finding
your bed empty?

Don't I talk with you
in the sharp cries of falcons?
Don't I look into your eyes
from the matt, white pages?

Why do you circle round,
the silent house like a thief?
Or do you remember the agreement
and wait for me alive?

I am falling asleep. The moon's blade
cuts through the stifling dark.
Again hoofbeats. It is my own warm
heart that beats so.

[1914]

'He was jealous, worried and tender'

He was jealous, worried and tender,
like God's sun he loved me,
but he killed my white bird
to stop it singing of the past.

Coming into the front room at sunset, he said:
'Love me, laugh, write poetry!'
I buried the happy bird
beyond the round well near the old alder tree.

I promised him not to cry,
but my heart turned to stone,
and it seems that always, and everywhere
I will hear its sweet voice.

[1914]

'How can you look at the Neva'

How can you look at the Neva,
how can you go out on the bridges?
There are good reasons I am called sad
since you first appeared.
The wings of black angels are sharp,
the last judgement is near
and the crimson bonfires,
like roses, bloom in the snow.

[1914]

Parting

Evening: a sloping
path before me.
Only yesterday, in love –
he implored, 'Don't forget.'

Now there are only the winds
and the cries of the shepherds,
the cedars in an uproar
by the clear springs.

[1914]

'The seaside garden road is dark'

The seaside garden road is dark.
The lamps are yellow and fresh.
I am very calm. Only do not
talk to me about him.
You are sweet and true – we will be friends...
Have fun, kiss, grow old...
And easy months will fly past
like the snowy stars above us.

[1914]

'Frosty sun'

Frosty sun. The troops
from the parade are marching, marching.
I am happy with the January noon,
and my worries are few.

I remember every twig
and silhouette here.
Crimson light drops
through frost's network.

The nearly white, glass-porched,
house was here, and
I held the bell ring in my lifeless
hand, so many times.

So many times...Play on, soldiers,
and I will search for my house;
I will recognise it by the sloping roof,
and the eternal ivy.

But someone moved it away,
carried it off to other towns,
or excised from the memory forever
the road that led there...

In the distance the bagpipes die away,
snow flies like cherry blossom on the wind,
and it is obvious that nobody knows
there is no white house.

[1914]

'"Tall woman, where is your gipsy boy"'

'Tall woman, where is your gipsy boy,
who cried under the black shawl,
where is your small first-born,
what do you know of him, what do you remember?'

'A mother's fate is a blessed torture,
I was not worthy of it.
The wicket gate into white paradise was unlocked,
Magdalene took my little boy.

I lost myself in the long spring
and every day is happy and good,
Yet still my arms mourn for their burden,
yet still I hear his crying in my sleep.

My heart becomes uneasy, weary,
and then I remember nothing.
I wander around the dark rooms,
I constantly search for his cradle.'

[1914]

'We thought: we're poor'

We thought: we're poor, we have nothing,
but when we started losing one after the other
so each day became
remembrance day,
we started composing poems
about God's great generosity
and – our former riches.

[1915]

To N.G. Chulkova

In these days that come just before spring
the meadow rests under thick snow,
there is the droll, dry rustle of trees
and the warm wind, soft and resilient.
The body marvels at its lightness.
Your house is not familiar to you,
and the song that annoyed you before,
you sing again – with new emotion.

[1915]

Dream

I knew you were dreaming of me,
that's why I couldn't get to sleep.
The street lamp's opaque blue
showed me the road.

You saw the Tsaritsa's Garden,
the intricate white palace,
the black tracery of railings
beside the echoing stone steps.

You walked, not knowing the way,
and thought, 'Faster, faster.
If only I could find her.
I must not wake before I meet her.'

The sentry by the splendid gates
called out: 'Where are you going?'
The ice crunched and broke,
water blackened under foot.

This lake – you thought –
there is a little island in the lake...
Suddenly a blue flame
peeped out of the darkness.

In the hard light of meagre day
you woke up and groaned,
and for the first time
loudly called out my name.

[1915]

'I still see hilly Pavlovsk'

I still see hilly Pavlovsk,
languid and shady,
the round meadow, the still water,
I will never forget it.

As you enter through the iron gates:
a sudden blissful shudder,
you die, but you rejoice and rave,
or you live completely differently.

In the late autumn the wind wanders
fresh and sharp, happy in the wilderness.
Black firs covered in white frost
stand on thawing snow.

Brimming with the fever of delirium,
the sweet voice sings,
and on the Citharode's bronze shoulder
a red-breasted bird sits.

[1915]

'"Coorlee, coorlee!" The cranes call'

'Coorlee, coorlee!' The cranes call
their wounded friend
when the autumn fields
are crumbled and warm.

And I, ill, hear the calls,
the noise of golden wings
from out of the thick, low clouds
and the dense woods.

'It's time to fly, to fly
over field and river.
You can no longer sing,
you can no longer wipe
the tears from your cheek
with a feeble hand.'

[1915]

'You cannot get here'

You cannot get here
by boat or by cart.
Deep water
lies on rotten snow.
The country house is
besieged
on all sides.
Cast away
like Robinson
he goes to look at the sledge,
at the skis, the horse,
and, later, sits
on the sofa, waiting for me,
rips the rug in half
with his short spur.
The mirrors no longer see
his gentle smile.

'The Immortelle is pink'

The Immortelle is pink and withered.
Clouds are crudely stuck onto the fresh sky.
The leaves of the only oak in this park
are without colour and frail.

The rays of the sunset burn till midnight.
My seclusion comforts me.
God's birds talk to me about
the most tender, the always wonderful one.

I am happy. But what I hold most dear
are the sloping forest path,
the simple, slightly crooked bridge,
and that there are only a few days left to wait.

[1916]

'Everything promised him to me'

Everything promised him to me:
the faded, red horizon,
a sweet dream on Christmas Eve,
the bell-chimes carried on the wind at Easter,

the elegant willow switches,
waterfalls in the park,
two large dragonflies
on the rusty iron railings.

As I walked along the hot, stone
path over the hills
I could not but believe
that he would be friends with me.

[1916]

'One memory lies within me'

One memory lies within me
like a white stone in the well's depth.
I can't and don't want to fight it:
it is happiness and it is suffering.

It seems to me that the person who looks closely
into my eyes will see it immediately.
He will become sadder and more pensive
than someone listening to a sorrowful tale.

I know that the gods metamorphosed
men into objects but did not kill their consciousness.
You are metamorphosed into my memory
so that the miracle of sadness may live forever.

[Slepnyovo, Summer 1916]

'The town vanished'

The town vanished. The window
of the last house looked out, as if it were alive.
This place is completely unfamiliar,
there is a smell of burning in the dark field.

But when the hesitant moon
cut through the storm clouds
we saw a lame man making his way
up the hill, towards the forest.

It was terrifying that he outran
the troika with its well-fed, eager horses.
He stopped for a while and then
hobbled on under his heavy burden.

Suddenly he appeared
by our kibitka,*
his blue eyes gleamed like stars
illuminating his exhausted face.

I held out the baby to him,
he lifted his hand that bore shackle marks
and clearly pronounced this blessing:
'May your son live and be healthy.'

[1916]

* *Russian hooded sledge*

'It seems that the voice of man'

It seems that the voice of man
will never be heard here,
only the stone-age wind
beats on the black gates.

It seems to me that I alone
survived under this sky,
because I was the first who wished
to drink of death's wine.

[1917]

'Yes, I loved those gatherings'

Yes, I loved those gatherings at night:
on a small table the ice-cold glasses.
The subtle, fragrant, steam of black coffee,
the red fire's heavy winter heat,
the acrid literary joke,
and the first glance of a friend, embarrassed and terrifying.

[1917]

WAYSIDE GRASS

'How terribly my body changed'

How terribly my body changed,
my exhausted lips turned pale.
I didn't want such a death,
I made the wrong appointment.
It seemed to me there would be
thunder claps and lightning bolts
and a voice more powerful than joy
would come down to me like angels.

[1913]

'A string of small beads'

A string of small beads round the neck,
I hide my hands in a wide muff,
my eyes are vacant
and do not cry any more.

My face seems paler
from the lilac silk,
my straight fringe
almost touches my eyebrows.

This slow walk
is not like the freedom of flight,
it's as though there is a raft under my feet
instead of the parquet floor.

My pale lips are parted,
my troubled breathing is uneven,
and on my breast tremble
the flowers of a meeting that never was.

[1913]

'O God, I can forgive everything done against me'

....

O God, I can forgive everything done against me,
but I'd rather be a hawk and tear apart a lamb,
or be a snake and bite the sleepers in the field,
than be a man and see against my will
what people do and because of the shame and decay of it
not dare to lift up my eyes to the heavens.

[1916(?)]

'The world's fame is like smoke'

The world's fame is like smoke —
I didn't ask for this.
I brought happiness
to all my lovers.
One's still alive,
in love with his love,
and another has become bronze
on the snowbound square.

[1914]

'I'd have thought you might come into my dreams less'

I'd have thought you might come into my dreams less,
after all we're seeing each other often.
But it's only in the sanctuary of darkness
that you are sad, emotional, tender,
and the endearing things you say
are sweeter than the Seraphim's praise.
It's only there that you don't sigh,
only there, that you don't mix up my name.

[1914]

'You looked into my face'

You looked into my face, then,
like an angel disturbing the water,
and brought back strength, and freedom,
and took as a memento of the miracle — my ring.
Melancholy prayers quenched
the burning fever of my disease.
I will remember the month of snowstorms.
An anxious February in the North.

[Tsarskoye Selo, February 1916]

'And I alone remained'

And I alone remained
to count the empty days.
O my free friends,
o my swans.

I won't bring you together in a song,
I won't return you in tears,
but in the sad evening hour
I will remember you in my prayers.

One of you fell,
struck by a deadly arrow,
and another kissed me
and turned into a black crow.

But this is how it is, once a year
when the ice melts
I stand by the clear waters
in the Tsaritsa's Garden

and hear the splash of broad wings
on the smooth blue lake.
I do not know who opened a window
in the grave's dungeon.

[1916]

'I will not speak to anyone'

I will not speak to anyone for a week.
I just sit on a rock by the sea.
It pleases me that the waves' green spray
is as salty as my tears.
Springs and winters have passed, but
I only remembered a certain spring.
The nights became warmer, the snow began to thaw.
I went out to look at the moon.
Seeing me alone in the pine forest
a stranger asked me quietly:
'Are you the one I searched for everywhere,
who has had for me, since my infancy
the happiness and sadness of a dear sister?'
I answered the stranger, 'No!'
But when the light from the heavens shone on him
I gave him my hands.
He gave me a mysterious ring
as a talisman against love
He named four special places
where we must meet again:
the sea, the round bay, the tall lighthouse,
and – most importantly – the wormwood tree.
Let my life end as it began,
I have told what I know: Amen.

[Sebastopol, 1916]

'I did not draw the curtains'

I did not draw the curtains,
you can look straight in to the drawing-room.
The reason I am happy
is that you cannot get away.
Call me immoral,
mock me cruelly:
I was your sleeplessness,
I was your anguish.

[1916]

'This meeting has been sung by no one'

This meeting has been sung by no one,
and without songs the sadness has died down.
Cool summer has come,
as though a new life has begun.

The sky seems to be a stone vault
wounded by the yellow flames.
More than my daily bread
I need one word, one word about him.

Enliven my soul with some news,
like the dew sprinkling the grass,
not for passion or for pleasure,
but for the sum of the world's love.

[Slepnyovo, 1916]

'I waited in vain for him'

I waited in vain for him for many years,
and it was as though I was asleep.
Three years ago on Palm Sunday
an eternal light shone.
I suddenly fell silent.
The bridegroom stood before me, smiling.

Outside the window people with candles walked slowly.
O that devout evening!
The thin April ice cracked slightly,
and the bells rang out over
the crowd like a prophetic comforting,
and a black wind flickered the little flames.

I saw as in a dawn haze
the white narcissi on the table,
the red wine in the cut-glass goblet.
My hand, spotted with wax,
trembled as he kissed it,
and my blood sang: 'Blessèd are you, celebrate!'

[1916]

'Both of us so quiet now'

Both of us so quiet now,
we are walking in tender silence
along the firm crest of the snowdrift
to my mysterious white house,
This fulfilled dream
is sweeter than all songs ever sung:
the brushing of twigs,
the clink of your spurs.

[January 1917]

'When the news finally reaches him'

When the news finally reaches him
of my bitter death,
he will not become more stern or sad,
but will turn pale and smile drily.

Then he'll suddenly remember the winter sky
and the snowstorm's rushing down the Neva,
and he'll suddenly remember how he swore
to look after his Eastern love.

[1917]

'So now farewell, my Petersburg'

So now farewell, my Petersburg,
farewell my spring.
The land of Karelia is
missing me.

The fields and back gardens
are calm and green.
The waters are still deep
and the skies pale.

The marsh water-nymph,
mistress of these parts,
looks, sighing pitifully,
at the cross on the bell-tower.

The oriole, friend
of my innocent days,
returned yesterday from the south,
cries among the branches:

that it is a shame to stay
in the cities till May,
to stifle in the theatre,
to be bored on the islands.

But the oriole does not know,
the water-nymph cannot understand
how sweet it is for me
to kiss him!

And yet I will go away
on the quiet slope
of today. Land of our Lord,
take me to yourself.

[1917]

'To wake up at dawn'

To wake up at dawn
smothering from joy's perfume
and look through the cabin window
at the green waves.
On deck in foul weather
wrapped in a fur coat
listening to the engine's thud.
Not to think about anything,
but anticipating meeting him,
who has become my star,
and grow younger each hour
from the salt spray and wind.

[1917]

'I walked with a light step'

I walked with a light step
into a secret friendship with the tall man,
dark-eyed as a young eagle,
as if into a flower garden before the coming of autumn.
The last roses were in bloom,
and the transparent moon was lulled
on thick, grey clouds.

[St Petersburg, June 1917]

'Suddenly it became quiet in the house'

Suddenly it became quiet in the house,
the last poppy's petals had scattered.
I feel drowsy,
and darkness comes early to me.

The gates are locked securely,
the evening is black, the wind is quiet.
where's the joy, the caring,
where are you my tender bridegroom?

Hasn't the secret ring been found?
I've waited for many days.
Like a tender prisoner
the song has died in my heart.

[1917]

'There is a troubled, uneasy hour'

There is a troubled, uneasy hour
like this every day.
I talk aloud with my anguish,
my sleepy eyes closed.
It thuds like the blood,
warm breathing,
like a happy love,
rational and cruel.

[1917]

'Oh no, burnt by a sweet fire'

Oh no, burnt by a sweet fire,
I didn't love you,
so just explain to me what power
your sad name holds over me.

You knelt before me,
as though you were waiting for the wedding crown,
and the shadows of death
touched your calm, young face.

90

You went away, not seeking victory
but death. The nights are deep.
O my angel, don't see, don't ever know
my present anguish.

But if the path in the forest
will be illuminated by the white sun of paradise,
but if the bird of the field
will fly from the twined sheaf,

I will know that you have been killed,
and have come to tell me about that,
and again I'll see the pock-marked hill
by the bloodied Dnester river.

I will forget the days of love and glory,
I will forget even my youth,
the soul is dark, the paths are treacherous,
but I will preserve your image and heroic quest
till the hour of death.

[Summer 1917]

'I don't like flowers'

I don't like flowers – they remind me
of funerals, weddings and balls,
and tables laid for dinner parties.

. . . .

But the simple beauty of everlasting roses,
which I always delighted in as a child,
has remained, like the music of Mozart,
my only inheritance...

[Tsarskoye Selo, 1910s]

'It's simple'

It's simple, it's quite clear,
everyone can understand it:
you don't love me at all,
you will never love me.
Why am I so drawn
to a man who belongs to someone else?
Why do I pray for you
every evening?
Why did I leave my love,
and the curly-haired child,
abandon my belovèd city
and the place I call home,
and wander around a foreign capital
like a downtrodden beggarwoman?
But the thought that I will see you
is so good!

[Summer 1917]

'The river flows without hurry'

The river flows without hurry down the valley.
The house on the hill has many windows.
And we live as in the time of Catherine the Great,
go to prayers, wait for the harvest.
The guest rides to us along the golden cornfield,
having endured two days of parting.
He kisses grandma's hand in the drawing-room
and my lips on the steep staircase.

[Summer 1917]

'For a whole day'

For a whole day, fearing its own groans
the crowd tosses in anguish.
Over the river on funeral banners
malevolent skulls laugh.
My heart was split in two
this is why I sang and dreamt.
With the sudden quiet after the gunshots
death sent patrols from yard to yard.

[1917]

'When the people waited'

When the people waited
in suicidal despair for the German visitors
and the stern spirit of Byzantium
had flown from the Russian Church,
when the capital by the Neva
had forgotten its greatness
and like a drunken whore
did not know who would take her next,
I heard a voice call consolingly,
'Come here, leave
your god-forsaken country,
abandon Russia for ever.
I'll wash the blood from your hands,
rip the black shame from your heart,
and give you a new name to cover
the pain of defeat and humiliation.'
But quite calmly, quite impartially,
I put my hands over my ears,
that my grieving spirit
should not be defiled by those shameful words.

[1917]

'Now no one will listen to songs and poems'

Now no one will listen to songs and poems.
The days that were foretold have come to pass.
My last song: the world holds no more miracles,
don't burst, my heart, don't resonate.

So recently your morning flight
was free as a swallow,
but now you will be a hungry beggar woman
and your knocking will not be answered at the strangers' gates.

[1917]

At Night

The moon hangs in the sky, scarcely alive
among the streaming, shallow cloud.
The gloomy sentry at the palace
looks crossly at the clock-tower hands.

An unfaithful wife is going home,
with a pensive, stern expression on her face,
and an insuppressible worry gnaws at
the faithful one in sleep's tight embrace.

What have I to do with them? Seven days ago
I sighed and said farewell to the world,
but it was stifling there and I went out into to the garden
to look at the stars and to touch the lyre.

[Moscow, Autumn 1918]

94

'When the moon does not roam'

When the moon does not roam in the sky,
but is the frozen seal of the night...
then my dead husband comes
to read my love letters.

He remembers the secret lock
on the carved oak chest.
The shackles on his legs
clank coarsely on the parquet floor.

He checks the dates of meetings
and the confusing patterns of signatures.
Has he not suffered
enough up till now?

[1910s]

'I asked the cuckoo'

I asked the cuckoo
how many years I would live...
The pine tops trembled,
a yellow shaft of sunlight fell to the grass.
There is no sound in the fresh forest depth...
I am going home,
and the cold wind caresses
my hot brow.

[1919]

'Why is this century worse'

Why is this century worse than those that have gone before?
In a stupor of sorrow and grief
it located the blackest wound
but somehow couldn't heal it.

The earth's sun is still shining in the West
and the roofs of towns sparkle in its rays,
while here death marks houses with crosses
and calls in the crows and the crows fly over.

[1919]

ANNO DOMINI

Lullaby

'Far away in a huge forest,
by the blue rivers,
lived a poor woodsman with his children
in a dark hut.

The youngest son was a tiny child.'
Hush now, my baby,
sleep my quiet one, sleep my little boy –
I am a bad mother.

News seldom gets through to our house
but we did hear that
your father got
the little white cross.

There were hard times and there will be again,
no end to the hard times –
let Saint George protect
your father.

[c. 1915]

Little Song

In the morning I used to keep quiet
about what my dream had sung to me.
The flushed rose, the sunbeam
and I share the same fate.
Snow slides from the sloping hills,
I am whiter than snow,
but I dream sweetly of the banks
of flooding, turbulent rivers.
The fresh murmur of a fir thicket
is more peaceful than waking thoughts.

[1916]

98

'A blackened and twisted log bridge'

A blackened and twisted log bridge.
The burdocks stand as tall as a man.
The dense nettle forests sing
that the scythe will not flash through them.
In the evening over the lake a sigh is heard,
rough moss has crawled over the walls.

There I was
twenty-one.
The black, choking honey
was sweet to the lips.

The twigs tore
my white silk dress,
the nightingale sang unceasingly
on the crooked pine.

At a given call
he would come out of hiding,
like a wild wood-spirit,
but more tender than a sister.

We ran to the mountain,
we swam across the river,
then afterwards,
I would not say leave me.

[1917]

'You thought I was that type'

You thought I was that type:
that you could forget me,
and that I'd plead and weep and throw myself
under the hooves of a bay mare,

D

or that I'd ask the sorcerers
for some magic potion made from roots
and send you a terrible gift:
my precious perfumed handkerchief.

Damn you! I will not grant
your cursed soul vicarious tears or a single glance.
And I swear to you by the garden of the angels,
I swear by the miracle-working ikon,
and by the fire and smoke of our nights:
I will never come back to you.

[July 1921]

'Terror, rummaging through things in the dark'

Terror, rummaging through things in the dark,
aims a moonbeam at an axe.
A sinister thud from behind the wall –
what's there, rats, a ghost, or a thief?

It splashes like water in the claustrophobic kitchen,
counts the shaky floorboards
it flashes past the attic window
with a glossy, black beard,

then silence. How evil and crafty is terror,
it hid the matches and blew out the candle.
I'd rather the gleam of the rifle
barrels aimed at my breast,

rather lie down on the unpainted scaffold
on the green square
and for my life blood to flow out
to the groans and screams of joy of the crowd.

I press the smooth crucifix to my breast:
O God, bring peace back to me.
The sweet smell of decay wafts
in a swoon from the cool sheet.

[Tsarskoye Selo, 27–28 August 1921]

'A pine bedstead'

A pine bedstead –
an iron enclosure.
How sweet that there is no longer
any need for me to be ·jealous.

They make up the bed for me
with weeping and with prayer,
now gallivant round the world
where you want, let God take care of you!

Now my hysterical outbursts will not
wound your hearing,
and the candle will not
burn through the night.

We have attained peace
and days of innocence...
You are crying – I am not worth
one of your tears.

[1921]

Slander

Slander accompanied me everywhere.
I heard its stealthy steps in my sleep,
and in the dead city under the merciless sky,
as I randomly searched for shelter and food.
Reflections of it burned in everyone's eyes,
either as betrayal, or as innocent terror.
I don't fear it. At every new challenge
I have a worthy and stern reply.
But I already foresee an inescapable day:
my friends will come to me at dawn
and trouble my sweetest sleep with sobbing,

and place an ikon on my cold chest.
Unknown to anyone slander will enter my blood.
Its insatiable mouth will not tire
of counting non-existent offences,
weaving its voice into the prayers of the requiem.
Its shameful delirium will be intelligible to all,
so then neighbour cannot look at neighbour,
then my body will remain in terrible emptiness,
then for the last time my soul will burn
with earthly weakness, flying in the dawn haze,
and burn in wild pity for the earth it has left.

[1921]

Black Dream

1.

He who praised me so awkwardly
still stomped around off-stage.
We were all, of course, happy to get away
from the blue-grey smoke and dim fire.

But a question burned in the confused words,
why did I not become a star of love?
The cruel, bloodless countenance hovering over us
was changed by the shameful pain.

Love me, remember, and cry!
Are not those who cry all equal before God?
Farewell! Farewell! The executioner will lead me
before dawn down the pale-blue roads.

2.

You are always mysterious, and new.
I submit to you more each day.

But your love, my stern friend
is an ordeal by steel and fire.

You forbid songs, poetry, and smiles
and, long ago, you forbade prayers.
Let's just never part,
you couldn't care about anything else!

So a stranger to earth and heaven,
I live and my songs have died,
as though you ripped away my free soul
from both heaven and hell.

[December 1917]

3.

Your enigmatic love
makes me scream in pain.
I turn pale, am prone to fainting,
my knees give way.

Don't hum any new songs,
they cannot deceive for long.
Claw with your claws more furiously
into my consumptive chest,

so that the blood would gush
from my throat onto the bed,
so death could once and for all rip from
my heart the forever cursed intoxication.

[July 1918]

4.

Ice blocks drift and clink,
the skies are hopelessly pale.
Oh why do you punish me?
I don't understand my guilt.

Kill me if necessary,
but don't be hard on me.
You don't want children from me
and you don't like my poems.

Have it your way then,
I kept my vow,
I gave you my life – but this sadness
I take with me to the grave.

[April 1918]

5. *Third Zachatevsky*

Backstreet, back...
The noose is tight round my throat.

A fresh breeze blows off the Moscow River,
the lamps in the windows are warm.

On the left – the waste land,
on the right – the monastery,

and opposite – the tall maple,
crimson in the red glow,

and opposite – the tall maple
hears a long groan at night.

The rotten street lamp squinted,
the bell-ringer returns from the church.

I wish I could find that ikon,
because my time is near.

I wish I had my black shawl again,
and a drink of Neva water.

[1940]

6.

I, obey you? Are you out of your mind!
I only obey the Lord's will.
I don't want trembling or pain,
my husband is my executioner, and his home the prison.

But as you see, it was I who came;
It was the very beginning of December, the wind howled in the
       fields.
It was so bright in your captivity,
and darkness stood guard outside the window.

So a bird beats with its whole body
against the transparent glass in the winter's foul weather,
and blood stains its white wing.

Now I am calm and happy,
farewell my quiet one, you are eternally dear to me
because you let a pilgrim into your home.

[August 1921]

'I am not among those who left our land'

I am not among those who left our land
to be torn to pieces by our enemies.
I don't listen to their vulgar flattery,
I will not give them my poems.

But the exile is for ever pitiful to me,
like a prisoner, like a sick man.
Your road is dark, wanderer;
alien corn smells of wormwood.

But here, stupefied by fumes of fire,
wasting the remainder of our youth,
we did not defend ourselves
from a single blow.

We know that history
will vindicate our every hour...
There is no one in the world more tearless,
more proud, more simple than us.

[1922]

'The swans are carried on the wind'

The swans are carried on the wind,
the blue sky is bloodied.
The anniversary of the first days
of your love approaches.

You destroyed my powers,
the years flowed like water.
Why haven't you grown old,
but remain as you were then?

Your tender voice rings even clearer,
only your trouble-free brow
has been shadowed with snowy distinction
by the wing of time.

[1922]

'If only I could fall ill in earnest'

If only I could fall ill in earnest, could meet
everyone again in a blazing delirium,
and walk down broad avenues
in the sunny wind-filled garden by the sea.

Now even the dead agree to come
and exiles live in my house.
Lead the child to me by the hand,
I have missed him for so long.

106

I will eat blue grapes with my darlings.
I will drink iced wine,
and watch the grey waterfall stream over
onto the wet flints — beneath.

[1922]

Biblical Poems

1. *Rachel*

And Jacob served seven years for Rachel;
and they seemed unto him but a few days,
for the love he had to her.
                    Genesis 29. 20

And Jacob met Rachel in the valley,
and bowed to her like a homeless pilgrim.
The flocks stirred up the hot dust,
the well was covered by a huge stone.
He rolled the stone off alone
and watered the sheep with the clean water.

But his heart started to grieve in his breast,
to ache, like an open wound,
and he agreed to serve seven years
for the girl, as a shepherd for Laban.
Rachel! For one in your power,
seven years are like seven radiant days.

But silver-loving Laban is more than wise,
and he knows no mercy.
He thinks to himself: any deception can be excused
for the glory of the house of Laban.
And he leads blind Leah with a firm hand
to Jacob's bridal chamber.

The lofty night streams over the desert,
and cool dew falls.

Laban's youngest daughter groans
and tears at her disarrayed hair.
She curses her sister and abuses God,
and orders the Angel of Death to appear.

And Jacob dreams of a short sweet time:
a clear well in the valley,
happy looks from Rachel's eyes
and her dove voice:
'Jacob, was it not you who kissed me
and called me your little black dove?'

[1921]

2. Lot's Wife

> But his wife looked back from behind him,
> and she became a pillar of salt.
>   Genesis 19. 26

The righteous man, huge and radiant, followed
the messenger of God over the black mountain.
But Anxiety spoke loudly to his wife:
'It's not too late, you can still look

at the fine red towers of your native Sodom,
at the square where you sang, at the courtyards where you spun
         wool,
at the empty windows of the tall house,
in which you bore children for your dear husband.'

She looked – and shackled by the agony of death,
her eyes could no longer look;
and her body became translucent salt,
and her swift feet were rooted to the ground.

Who will mourn this woman in song?
Is she not thought of as the most insignificant of losses?
Only my heart will never forget
her, who gave her life for a single glance.

[1922–1924]

3. *Michal*

I Samuel 18. 20

And the young man plays to the mad king
and destroys the merciless night,
and loudly calls up the victorious dawn
and suffocates the apparitions of horror.
And the king speaks to him graciously:
'Young man, a wondrous flame burns within you,
and for such healing medicine
I will give you my youngest daughter in marriage, and my
          kingdom.'
And the king's daughter looks at the singer,
she needs no songs, wedding or crown,
her heart is mournful and resentful,
but Michal wants David.
She is paler than the dead, her lips are pursed;
her green eyes are wild;
her clothes shine, her bracelets
ring delicately at her every move;
like a secret, like a dream, like the earth's first mother Lilith.

She speaks without her own will:
'They must have put poison in my drink
and my spirit is growing dim.
My shame! My humiliation!
Tramp! Robber! Shepherd!
Oh, why aren't any of the nobles
at court like him?
But the rays of the sun...the stars at night...
This shudder down the spine.'

[1922–1961]

'That fantastic autumn'

That fantastic autumn built a dome.
The clouds were ordered not to darken the dome.
The people marvelled: September is passing
and where are the chill, damp days?
The murky canal waters turned emerald,
the nettles smelled like roses, only more intense.
It was stifling with sunsets: unbearable, devilish, crimson,
we will all remember them till the end of our days.
The sun was like a rebel entering the capital,
and the spring-like autumn caressed the frail snowdrop so
        passionately
that it seemed it would blossom white.
That was when you, cool and calm, came to my door.

[1922]

'It is good here'

It is good here: rustle and snow-crunch,
the frost is fiercer every morning,
a bush of blinding ice roses
bows in white flame.
Ski tracks on the splendid finery
of the snow: a memory
that long ages ago
we passed here together.

[1922]

110

New Year Ballad

And the moon, weary in the pall of cloud,
cast a murky glance into the room,
where the table is laid for six
with only one place empty.

My husband, my friends and myself
are celebrating the new year.
Why do my fingers seem bloody?
Why does the wine burn like poison?

The host with full glass raised,
was impressive and immobile.
'I drink to the earth of our own forest glades,
in which we all rest.'

A friend looked at my face,
and suddenly remembering God knows what,
exclaimed: 'I drink to her songs
in which we all live!'

But a third, not understanding,
as he went out into the dark,
answering my thoughts
said: 'We ought to drink to him
who is not with us yet.'

[1923]

'The ale is brewed'

The ale is brewed,
the steaming goose is on the table...
Russia is about to celebrate
and remember the Tsar and the landowner –

with strong words, with witty phrases
in a tipsy conversation:
one with a *risqué* joke,
one with a drunken tear.

The wine and carousal
carry off the noisy speeches...
The clever ones have decided:
our place is on the sidelines.

[Bezhetsk, Christmas 1921]

To Many

I am your voice, the heat of your breathing,
I am the reflection of your face,
the quiverings of helpless wings are hopeless.
You know I really am with you till the end.

This is why you love me so greedily
in my sin and powerlessness.
This is why you gave me the birthright
of your best son.
That's why you never asked
me even a word about him,
but filled my deserted home
with the noxious smoke of praise.
People say: they couldn't be closer,
one couldn't love more totally...

As the shadow wishes to separate from the body,
and the flesh wishes to part from the soul,
so now, I want to be – forgotten.

[September 1922]

REED

Inscription in a Book
To M.L. Lozinsky

From a shade almost beyond the Lethe,
in the hour when worlds are being destroyed,
take this gift of spring
in response to your own best gifts,
so that high freedom of the soul,
undefeatable and true,
above all seasons,
which is called friendship
may smile to me as tenderly
as thirty years ago...
The railings in the Summer Garden
and snowbound Leningrad
arose as in this book,
from the magic mirror's haze,
and over the pensive Lethe,
the reed pipe came to life and played.

[May 1940]

The Muse

In the night when I wait for her to come
life seems to hang on a strand of hair.
What are honours, what is youth, what is freedom
before the dear guest with the little flute in her hand?

There, she has entered. She threw back her veil
and looked at me inquisitively.
I ask her: 'Was it you who dictated
to Dante the pages of *Inferno*?' She answers: 'It was I.'

[1924]

114

To the Artist

Your work still haunts me,
your blessed labours:
the gilt of the forever autumnal, lime trees,
and the blue of water, created today.

Think, even the shallowest daydream
leads me to your gardens,
where, in fear at each turn,
I search for your tracks deliriously.

Will I enter under the vault
metamorphosed by your hand into sky,
so that my cursed fever could be cooled?

There I'll be blessed for eternity,
and closing my scorched eyelids
I shall find once more the gift of tears.

[1924]

'One can leave this life so simply'

One can leave this life so simply
and burn out without thought or pain,
but the Russian poet is not fated
to die an untroubled death.

It's much more likely that a bullet will take
his winged soul across the border to heaven
or the hairy paws of hoarse terror will squeeze
the life from his heart — as though it were a sponge.

[1925]

'Forgive me that I am coping badly'

Forgive me that I am coping badly,
coping badly, yet I live in a holy light.
I'll leave a memory of myself in songs and poems,
but you dreamed of me in reality.
Forgive me, although you do not know yet
that ambiguous slanders are combined
with my name for ever,
as acrid smoke is with joyful fire.

[1927?]

'Here Pushkin's exile began'

Here Pushkin's exile began
and Lermontov's ended.
Here are the fragrant mountain grasses.
And only once did I actually see
under the deep shade of the plane tree, by the lake,
in that cruel hour before evening,
the shining unsatisfied eyes
of the demon.

[Kislovodsk, 1927]

'If the moon's horror splashes'

If the moon's horror splashes,
the whole city is in a poisonous solution.
Without the slightest hope of going to sleep,
through the green fog
I do not see my childhood, nor the sea,

nor the butterflies' wedding flight
over the bed of snow-white narcissi,
in nineteen sixteen...
but the eternally petrified round dance
of the cypresses over your grave.

[1 October 1928]

'That city that I have loved'

That city that I have loved since I was a child
seemed to me today
in its December stillness
to be my squandered inheritance.

Everything that was handed to me spontaneously,
was so easy to give away:
the soul's burning heat, the sounds of prayer,
and the grace of the first song —

all, all carried away in transparent smoke,
turned to ash in the depths of mirrors...
and now a noseless violinist
strikes up a tune from the irrevocable past.

With the curiosity of a foreigner
captivated by everything new
I listened to my Mother Tongue
and watched the sledges race.

Happiness blew in my face
with a wild freshness and force,
as though an eternally dear friend
accompanied me onto the steps.

[1929]

Couplet

For me, praise from others is like ash,
from you, even abuse is praise.

[1931]

Incantation

From the tall gates,
from the marshes beyond the Okhta,
by an untrod path,
by the unscythed meadow,
through the cordon of night,
under the Easter peal,
uninvited,
not my fiancé,
come to me for supper.

[1935]

'Wild honey'

Wild honey smells of freedom,
dust of sunbeams,
a young girl's breath of violets,
and gold – of nothing.
Mignonette smells of water,
of apples – love.
But we have found out forever
that only blood smells of blood.

In vain the Roman proconsul
washed his hands before the multitude
to the malevolent screams of the rabble;
and the Scottish queen
in vain kept rubbing the red spots
from her slender palms
in the choking darkness of the king's house...

[1933]

'Why did you poison the water'

Why did you poison the water
and mix my bread with dirt?
Why do you turn remnants of
freedom into a robbers' den?
Because I didn't violently curse
the bitter fate of friends,
because I stayed faithful
to my sad homeland?
Let it be so. The poet cannot exist
on this earth without the executioner's block.
Our fate is to wear the shirts of the penitent,
and to carry the candle and howl.

[1935]

'Didn't he send a swan for me'

Didn't he send a swan for me,
or a boat, or a black raft?
In the spring of nineteen sixteen
he promised he would come soon.
In the spring of nineteen sixteen
he said I would fly like a bird,

through the dark and death, to his chamber
and touch his shoulder with my wing.
His eyes still laugh at me
even now, sixteen springs later.
What can I do? The midnight angel
talks with me till dawn.

[Moscow 1936]

'Some mirror themselves in lovers' eyes'

Some mirror themselves in lovers' eyes,
others drink till the sun rises,
but I hold peace talks all night
with my indomitable conscience.

I say to her: 'Do you know how many years
I have been carrying your heavy burden?'
But time does not exist for her,
and for her there is not enough space in this world.

Again the black carnival evening,
the sinister park, the unhurried pace of the horse,
and the wind full of fun and happiness
blowing on me from the heavens' height.

Hanging over me, the witness, serene,
two-horned moon...Oh to go there, to go there
along the ancient track to the gazebo in the park
and the swans and the dead waters of the lake.

[1936]

'I hid my heart from you'

I hid my heart from you
as though I'd hurled it in the Neva.
I live in your home,
tamed, wingless.
Only, I hear squeaks in the night.
What's there in the strange twilight?
The Sheremetev lime trees...
The crosscalling of house spirits...
The black soft whisper of disaster
cautiously creeps up,
like water burbling along,
leans feverishly over me
and mutters in my ear,
as though it's on night duty here:
'You wanted comfort,
now do you know where that comfort is?'

[30 October 1936]

Boris Pasternak

He who compared himself to a horse's eye,
squints, looks, sees, recognises,
and already the puddles shine
like a fused diamond, the ice pines away.

The backwoods rest in a lilac haze,
platforms, logs, leaves, clouds,
the engine whistles, the crunch of melon peel,
a timid hand in a fragrant kid glove.

There is a ringing, a thundering, a gnashing, the crash of surf,
and then suddenly quiet: this means
he is treading the pine needles, fearful lest
he should scare awake the light dream-sleep of space.

This means he is counting the grains
in the empty ears; this means
he has come again from some funeral
to the cursed, black, Daryal Gorge.

Moscow languor burns again,
death's little bells ring in the distance –
Who has got lost two steps from home,
where the snow is waist deep and an end to everything?

For comparing smoke with Laocoön,
for singing of the graveyard thistle,
for filling the earth with a new sound
in a new space of mirrored stanzas,

he is rewarded with a form of eternal childhood,
with the bounty and vigilance of the stars,
the whole world was his inheritance
and he shared it with everyone.

[19 January 1936]

Voronezh
Osip Mandelstam

The town stands completely icebound.
Trees, walls, snow as though under glass.
Timidly I walk over the crystals.
The painted sledge jolts along.
In Voronezh there are crows over Peter's statue,
poplars and a verdigris dome,
eroded, in the turbulent sun-dust.
Here the slopes of the powerful earth still quake
from the victory over the Tatars at Kulikovo.
The poplars like glasses touching
will chime loudly,
as though one thousand guests were toasting
our triumph at a wedding feast.

While in the room of the exiled poet
fear ,and the Muse stand duty in turn
and the night is endless
and knows no dawn.

[1936]

Dante

> *Il mio bel San Giovanni*
> Dante's *Inferno*

He didn't return to his old city,
Florence, even after his death.
He did not look back as he went away,
and I sing this song to him.
Torches, night, the final embrace,
the wild shriek of fate beyond the threshold.
He sent a curse on her from hell
and could not forget her in heaven.
But never, in a penitent's shirt,
did he walk barefoot with a lighted candle
through his beloved Florence,
perfidious, base, longed for.

[17 August 1936]

A Little Geography
To Osip Mandelstam

Not as the capital of Europe
with the first prize for beauty –
but as an exile station to the choking Yenisey
with a transition on to Chita,
to Ishim, to waterless Irgiz,

to the famous Atbasar,
and all change for Freedom Camp,
to the corpse stink of rotted bunks –
that is how this city appeared to me
that sky-blue midnight,
that city sung of by the first poet,
by us sinners – and by you.

[1937]

Fragments of Pottery

> *You cannot leave your mother an orphan*
> Joyce

I.

For me, deprived of fire and water,
parted with my one and only son.
I stand, on the shameful scaffold of disaster
as if I were under the canopy of a throne.

II.

He who argued his way so violently – through
to the plains around the Yenisey...
To you he's a down-and-out, a Chouane, a conspirator,
to me he's my one and only son.

III.

You will not hear the mother calling
from seven thousand and three kilometres away
through the menacing howl of the Polar wind,
in the crush of disasters that surrounds you.
You my dear one are becoming a wild beast there,
you the last and the first, you are ours.
Dispassionate spring wanders
over my Leningrad grave.

124

IV.

I spoke to whomever, whenever;
why don't I hide the fact
that labour camp rotted my son,
that they whipped my Muse to death?
I am the most guilty person on earth –
in the past, in the present, and in the future.
and for me it is a great honour
to toss and turn in the madhouse.

V.

You will hoist me onto a bloody hook
like a slain beast,
so that foreigners giggling with disbelief
should wander around
and write in learned journals
that my incomparable gift had died;
that I was a poet of poets,
but that thirteen o'clock had struck for me.

[1930s/1940s]

Imitation of the Armenian

You will dream of me as a black ewe
on unsteady thin legs.
I'll come up, start bleating and crying:
'Did you dine well, Padishah?
You hold the universe in your hand like a bead,
and are preserved by the bright will of Allah...
And did my son, my little lamb, taste good
to you and your children?'

[1930s]

'Celebrate this, our last anniversary'

Celebrate this, our last anniversary,
realise that the snowy night
of our first diamond winter,
is exactly repeating itself tonight.

The smoke billows from the royal stables,
the Moyka river drowns in the dark.
The moonlight is dimmed as though on purpose
and where we are going I cannot tell.

Between graves of grandson and grandfather,
the Mikhailovsky Garden is overgrown.
The street lamps burn funereally,
as though they've surfaced from a prison delirium.

The Field of Mars is strewn with icebergs.
The Swan canal is in ice crystals.
If in my heart dwell joy and terror
whose fate could be compared with mine?

Your voice over my shoulder
trembles like a wondrous bird,
and caught in an incandescent sunbeam
the snow dust is like warm silver.

[1938]

'I know there's no moving'

....
I know there's no moving from the spot
under the weight of the eyelids of Gogol's Viy.
Oh, to escape back
into some sort of seventeenth century:

126

To stand in church at Whitsun
with a fragrant birch branch,
and drink sweet mead
with the noblewoman Morozova.

To go off afterwards, on a wood sledge at twilight,
and sink in the dung-spattered snow.
What mad Surikov
will paint my last journey?

[1939]

'Happy New Year!'

Happy New Year! What new troubles will it bring?
Look how it dances, mischievously,
over the smoking Baltic sea,
hobbling, hunchbacked and wild.
What lot did it cast
for the one who missed the torture cell?
They went out onto the field to die.
Shine on them the stars in the sky.
No more for them to see the bread
of the earth or loved ones' eyes.

[January 1940]

The Cellar of Memory

But it's absolute rubbish that I live in grief
and that a memory in the past gnaws at me.
It's not often I am memory's guest,
and it always makes a fool of me.

When I go down with a torch to the basement,
it seems to me that on the narrow stair
a dense avalanche thunders after me.
The torch splutters smoke, I cannot go back,
I know I am going to the enemy.
And I beg for mercy...however it's quiet
there and dark. My celebration is all over.
It's thirty years since they said farewell to ladies.
That playboy died of old age.
I was too late. What a disaster.
I can't appear anywhere – it's impossible.
But I touch the murals
and warm myself by the fire. What a miracle!
Through this mould, this smoke and decay,
two green emeralds flashed,
and a cat miaowed. Let's go home!

Am I losing my reason, as I have lost my home?

[18 January 1940]

'For all those'

For all those whom my heart will not forget,
but for some reason are nowhere,
and those children of terror
who will never live to see their twenties.
Eight years, nine years old –
and then...Enough, don't torture yourself.
All those whom you truly loved
will remain alive for you.

[1940]

Cleopatra

I am fire and air...
Shakespeare

She'd already kissed Antony's dead lips,
on her knees, before Augustus, she'd already shed tears...
The servants had betrayed her. The victory trumpets blare
under the Roman eagle and the evening mist spreads.

Tall, stately the last captive
of her beauty enters, and whispers in confusion:
'He will parade you before him in the Triumph like a slave girl.'
But her swan neck's curve is as calm as ever.

Tomorrow they'll put the children in chains. Oh how little
she had left to do on this earth – to joke with a simple countryman
and with an impassive hand to place on her dark breast,
in parting compassion, the little black snake.

[7 February 1940]

Stanzas

Night by the Moscow river. A Streltsy moon.
The Passion week hours pass like the Way of the Cross.
I am dreaming a fearful dream. Is it really true
that no one, no one, no one can help me?

One mustn't live in the Kremlin, Peter the Great is right.
There the microbes of ancient violence still seethe,
The wild terror of Boris, and all the Ivans' evil hatred,
the Pretender's arrogance, instead of the people's rights.

[1940]

129

'I put my curly-haired son to bed'

I put my curly-haired son to bed
and went to the lake to get water.
I sang songs. I was happy.
As I was drawing water I heard
a familiar sound:
bells ringing
under the blue waves:
as they rang for us in Kitezh city.
The big bells of St George's
and the little bells of the Church of the Annunciation
spoke to me in menacing tones:

'You alone escaped the attack.
You did not hear our groans,
you did not see our bitter destruction.
The eternal candle burns brightly
for you by the throne of the Almighty.
Why do you linger on earth
and not hasten to take the crown?
Your lily bloomed at midnight,
your bridal veil reaches the floor...
Why do you sadden your brother, the soldier,
and your dear sister, the nun,
and your little child?...'

When they'd finished speaking
I saw stars.
I looked round: my house was on fire.

[March 1940]

130

'So the dark souls fly off'

So the dark souls fly off.
Don't listen, let me rant on deliriously.

You came unexpectedly, without warning.
You are beyond time.

So stay with me a little longer.
Remember how we were together in Poland.

The first morning in Warsaw...Who are you?
Are you the second man, or the third? 'I am the hundredth!'

Your voice is the same as it was then.
You know I lived for years in the hope

that you'd come back, but now, I am unhappy,
I need nothing on this earth:

not Homer's thunderclaps, or Dante's divine miracle.
Soon I'll come out on the blessed shore

where Troy has not fallen and Enkidu is alive
and everything is suffused in fragrant mist.

I would doze under the green willow,
but these bells give me no peace.

What is it? Are the cattle returning from the mountain?
There's no cool evening breeze.

Or is the priest adminstering the sacrament?
The stars are in the sky and it's night over the mountains.

Or are they calling the people to congregate?
'No, it is your last evening!'

[1940]

E

'When a man dies'

When a man dies
his portraits change.
His eyes look in a different way,
his lips smile a different smile.
I noticed this on returning
from the funeral of a poet.
Since then I have often checked it,
and my theory has been confirmed.

[21 May 1940]

Willow

And a decrepit bunch of trees
Pushkin

I grew in patterned silence
in the cool nursery of the century.
Man's voice held no sweetness for me
but I understood the wind.
I loved the burdocks and the nettles
but above all the silver willow.
Thankful it lived with me
all its life, weeping branches
fanning sleeplessness with dreams.
Strange – I outlived it.
Now a stump sticks up there, other willows
say something in strange voices
under our unchanging heavens.
I am silent…as though my brother were dead.

[18 January 1940]

132

'The neighbour-woman, out of pity, will accompany me'

The neighbour-woman, out of pity, will accompany me for
        two blocks,
the old women, as is the custom, to the gates.
But the man whose hand I held
will go with me to the grave.
He will stand above the crumbly, black, native soil.
alone in this world.
He will call louder and louder,
but my voice will not answer him, as it did before.

[15 August 1940]

'So in defiance'

> *The trees in the forest vote*
> N. Zabolotsky

So in defiance
of death looking us in the eyes
again, as you foretold
I vote *for:*
door becoming door,
lock becoming lock,
the sullen beast becoming humane
in the chest. But the thing is that
we are all fated to learn
what it means not to sleep for three years,
what it means to find out in the morning
who has perished in the night.

[1940]

Splitting Up

1.

Not weeks, not months, years
of splitting up. Now finally
the chill of real freedom
as the temples go grey.

No more treachery or betrayals,
and you won't have to listen
till dawn to the overwhelming evidence
that I was always right.

[1942]

2.

And as always happens in the days of splitting up
the shadow of our first days knocked at the door.
The silver willow burst into
the grandeur of its grey branches.

To us who dare not lift our eyes from the ground,
to us proud, bitter and berserk,
a bird sang with blessed voice
about how we had looked after each other...

[25 September 1944]

3.   *Final Toast*

I drink to the home in ruins,
to my angry life,
to loneliness together,
and it's to you I drink —
to the lying lips that betrayed me,
to the deadly cold eyes,
to the fact that the world is cruel and coarse,
and that God did not save us.

[27 June 1934]

Mayakovsky in 1913

I didn't know you when you were famous,
I only remember your stormy dawn.
Perhaps today it's right to remember
a day in the remote past.
The sounds gathered strength in your poems,
the new voices swarmed in...
Your young hands were not lazy,
and you built menacing structures.
You seemed to transform
everything you touched.
What you destroyed, was utterly destroyed
and a death sentence rang in every sentence.
Not content with a twilight life
you accelerated fate through impatience,
knowing that you would soon emerge
happy and free for the great struggle.
When you read to us, even then, the echo
of the tide's roar was audible.
The rain slanted its eyes angrily,
you argued headlong with the city.
An as yet unheard of name flashed
like lightning in the stifling hall.
Now, honoured by the whole country,
your name is like a clarion call.

[1940]

Inscription in the Book *Wayside Grass*

I remember the humble wayside grass
from that distant, alien spring
and not that mysterious artist
who ploughed Hoffman's dreams.

135

It grew everywhere, the town was green with it,
it adorned the broad steps,
and Psyche returned to my sanctuary
bearing the torch that liberated my poetry.

In the depth of the fourth courtyard
the children danced gleefully by the tree
delighted by the one-legged organ grinder.
Life rang like a full peal of bells.
And my wild blood led me to you
down the one and only road that is everyone's fate.

[1941]

Leningrad in March 1941

A *Cadran Solaire** on the Menshikov house.
The boat leaves a wake as it passes.
Is there anything in this world more familiar to me
than the sparkle of spires reflected on this water?
The backstreet is dark as a mouse-hole.
The sparrows perch on the wires
by the walks rooted in the memory.
This salty taste doesn't necessarily mean disaster.

[1941]

*sun dial

SEVENTH BOOK

3. *The Muse*

How can I live with this burden
which they still call the Muse?
They say: 'You're with her on the meadow...'
They say: 'Divine babbling....'
She is crueller than a recurrent fever.
Again there's a whole year without a mutter or a murmur.

4. *The Poet*

You wouldn't think by the look of it
that this carefree life is work.
To eavesdrop on music
and jokingly pretend it is your own.

And when you've put into a poem
some happy scherzo,
to swear that your poor heart
is groaning with pain while you stand in the sunny field.

Then to eavesdrop on the forest,
on the pines which appear sworn to silence,
when the smoky veil
of mist hangs all around.

I take from the right, I take from the left,
and even without any feelings of guilt,
a little from crafty life,
and all from the stillness of night.

[Komarovo, Summer 1959]

5. *The Reader*

You must not be particularly unhappy,
and above all not secretive. Oh no!
The poet is wide open
to make himself clear to modern man.

The footlights illuminate from beneath,
everything is dead, empty and bright.
His brow is branded by the cold
flame of the limelight.

But each reader is like a secret,
like a treasure chest buried deep in the earth,
even if he is the least important, the least likely,
silent throughout life.

Everything that nature will hide from us,
when it suits her, is there.
There where someone cries helplessly
at an appointed hour,

where the night is dark,
and shadowy, and cool –
where those unknown eyes
talk with me till dawn.

They rebuke me for some things,
on others, they agree,
so the mute confession flows on:
the blessèd heat of a conversation.

Our life passes quickly on this earth,
and the predestined circle is tight,
and the unknown friend of the poet
is faithful, eternal.

[Komarovo, Summer 1959]

6. *Last Poem*

One poem thundering as if disturbed by someone,
bursts into my home breathing life,
laughs, vibrates near the throat,
circles and applauds.

Another poem, born of the midnight silence,
creeps up to me out of nowhere,
looks out of the empty mirror
and speaks to me softly and sternly.

There are others too that come in the middle of the day,
and stream onto the white paper
like a clear spring in a valley,
almost as if they hadn't seen me.

And yet another: a mysterious one that prowls about,
not a sound, not a colour, not a colour, not a sound,
it sets boundaries, changes, coils,
and won't give itself up alive.

But for me the worst disaster
is the poem that drank
blood drop by drop,
as a wicked young girl drinks love,

and not having said a word to me
it becomes the silence again.
It's gone and its tracks lead to some extreme extreme,
and without it – I die.

[Leningrad, 1 December 1959]

7. *Epigram*

Could Bice, the real Beatrice, compose like Dante,
or Petrarch's Laura glorify the heat of love?
I taught women to speak...
But, Lord, how can I force them to be quiet?

[1958]

8. *On Poetry*
To Vladimir Narbut

It is the husks of sleepless nights,
it is the congealed wax of crooked candles,
it is the first morning chime
of a hundred white bells...
It is the warm windowsill
under the Ukrainian moon,
it is bees, it is clover,
it is dust and gloom and intense heat.

[Moscow, April 1940]

9.

There are many more things
that cry out to become my poems:
that which thunders wordlessly,
and chisels in the dark at underground rock,
or bursts through the smoke.
My account with fire, wind,
and water is still unsettled,
and that's why my reverie
will suddenly throw wide the doors for me,
and lead me to follow the Morning Star.

[1942]

10. *'Quatrain'*

Your soul is rich, there's no need to repeat
that which has once been said.
But perhaps poetry itself
is just one glorious quotation.

'In books I always like the last page'

In books I always like the last page
much more than all the others,
when we're no longer interested
in hero or heroine, and so many years
have passed that one does not feel sorry for anyone,
and the author himself seems
to have forgotten the beginning of the story,
and even 'eternity has turned grey'
as someone puts it in some good book.
But now, now
everything will be over soon and the author
will be irrevocably alone again,
yet he still tries to be clever
or sarcastic, God forgive him,
and produce a flowery ending,
like this one for instance:
and in only two houses
in that city (name uncertain)
a profile remained (traced by
someone on the wall's snow-white wash),
neither of a woman, nor of a man, but full of mystery.
And they say, when the beams of the moon,
green, low, Central Asian,
run over these walls at midnight,
especially on New Year's Eve,
then some soft sound is heard,
in which some hear crying,
and others discern words.
But everyone grew tired of the miracle.
Few people come there nowadays, the locals are used to it,
and they say the cursed profile in one of those houses
is now covered by a rug hung on the wall.

[Tashkent, 25 November 1943]

Pushkin

Who knows what fame really means?
At what price did he buy the right,
the opportunity or grace
to make jokes so wisely and cunningly
at everyone's expense,
then to fall mysteriously silent
and to lovingly caress the word ankle?

[Tashkent, 7 March 1943]

'Our sacred craft'

Our sacred craft has existed
for thousands of years...
It is the light of the world even in the darkness.
But no poet has ever said
that there is no wisdom, no old age
and even, perhaps, no death.

[Leningrad, 25 June 1944]

In 1940

1.

When the epoch is buried
no psalm is sung over the grave.
Nettles and thistles will decorate it.
And only the gravediggers work strenuously,
for their work cannot wait.
And it's still, my God, so still,
that one can hear the footsteps of time.

Then the epoch emerges and floats
like a corpse on a river in spring.
The son will not recognise his mother
and the grandson will turn away in anguish.
Heads are bowed.
The pendulous moon moves on.
Paris is lost –
and we feel the silence.

[1940]

2. To the Londoners

Time is writing Shakespeare's twenty-fourth drama,
with a clear, dispassionate hand,
and for us, the partakers of this menacing feast,
it is better to read *Hamlet, Julius Caesar* or *King Lear*
by the molten lead river.
Better for us today to accompany the little dove Juliet
to the grave with torches and singing,
better to look through the window at Macbeth
and tremble with the hired murderer,
but not this, not this, not this,
this even we aren't capable of reading.

3. Shadow

> *What does a certain woman*
> *know about the hour of death?*
>   O. Mandelstam

You, always more elegant, taller than all of them, more like
            a rose,
why do you float up from the bottom of that dead age?
And my memory swooped on
your clear profile behind the carriage window.
Do you remember the arguments over whether you were a bird or
            an angel?
The poet called you a straw girl.
The tender light of your Georgian temptress eyes
looked the same through their black eyelashes at everyone.

146

O shadow! Forgive me, but sleeplessness,
Flaubert, clear weather and the late lilac
reminded me of you, the beauty of 1913, and brought back
your, cloudless, dispassionate day,
and, shadow, these kinds of memories
do not suit me.

4.

Didn't I know sleeplessness'
every pit and path?
But this is like the clatter of cavalry horses' hooves
to the wild howl of the trumpet.
I go into the deserted houses,
someone's recent shelters.
All is quiet, only white shadows
swim in foreign mirrors.
What's there in the mist,
Denmark or Finland?
Or have I been here before,
and is this a transcription
of those eternally forgotten minutes?

5.

But I warn you that
I am living for the last time.
Not as a swallow, not as a maple,
not as a reed or a star,
not as the spring water,
not as the bell tower chimes,
will I disturb anyone
and with an inconsolable groan
visit strangers' dreams.

[1940]

Wind of War

Wind of War

1. Oath

May she who says farewell to her dear one today,
convert her pain into strength.
We swear to our children, swear to the graves,
that no one will force us to submit!

[Leningrad, July 1941]

2. 'They said dramatic goodbyes'

They said dramatic goodbyes to their girlfriends,
and dressed up in new uniforms,
they kissed their mothers as they marched
away to play toy soldiers.
Not bad or good or mediocre,
they were all at their posts,
where no one is first or last...
They all went to their eternal rest.

[1943]

3. First Long Range Shelling of Leningrad

The quality of the city's hustle
and bustle suddenly changed.
This was neither a town
nor a country sound.
True, it was closely related
to claps of distant thunder,
but in thunder there is the wetness
of the high fresh clouds
and the longing of the meadows;
the news of the joyous cloudbursts.
But this sound was hot and dry as hell,
and my confused hearing did not want

to believe
how it spread and grew
and dispassionately brought destruction to
my child.

[September 1941]

4. 'Birds of death'

Birds of death hover in the zenith.
Who is coming to rescue Leningrad?

Don't make any noise — Leningrad is still breathing,
it's still alive, hears everything:

its sons on the Baltic sea bed
groaning in their sleep,

their screams from the depths: 'Bread!' —
reach that seventh paradise...

But the heavens are merciless.
Death looks out of all windows.

[September 1941]

5. Courage

We know what now lies in the balance
and what is coming to pass.
Courage's hour has struck —
courage will not fail us.
We are not afraid to face the bullets and die,
we are not bitter at being left homeless —
we will preserve you our Russian language,
the great Russian word.
Pure and free we will uphold you
and hand you on to our children's children,
and save you from captivity
            forever!

[23 February 1942]

150

6–7. *In Memory of a Leningrad boy,*
my neighbour Valya Smirnov

1.

The lights are out.
Trenches are dug in the garden.
Petersburg's orphans
are my little children –
one can't breathe underground,
pain drills the forehead.
Through the bombing
a child's small voice is heard.

2.

Knock with your little fist – I'll open up.
I always opened my door to you.
Now I've gone beyond the high mountain,
the desert, the wind and the blazing heat,
but I will never give you up...

I did not hear you crying
or asking me for bread.
Bring me a twig from the maple tree,
or just some blades of green grass
as you did last spring.
Bring me in your tiny cupped hands
some clear, cool water from our Neva,
and with my own hands I'll wipe clean
the blood from your little golden head.

[23 April 1942]

10. *'O you my friends who have just been called to battle'*

O you my friends who have just been called to battle!
My life has been saved so I can mourn you,
and not to freeze like a weeping willow over your memory,
but scream out your names to the whole world.

But names are not important!
                      I slam shut the prayer book
and everyone's on their knees!
                    The crimson light flares.
The living and the dead of Leningrad
file out: in fame no one is dead.

[1942]

11. *'To the right the waste land stretched'*

To the right the waste land stretched,
with the strip of the sunset as old as the world itself,

To the left the three streetlamps are like gallows
                  in a row...

The jackdaws' cry is everywhere.
The moon has risen without purpose –
its face is lifeless.

This is from a life that is not bound by time.
This is when the golden age will be.

This is when the battle will be over –
and when we two shall meet.

[Tashkent, 29 April 1944]

12–16. *Victory*

1.

The glorious labour is gloriously begun,
in the menacing thunder, in the snow dust
where the purest body of the motherland
lies, defiled by the enemy.

152

The dear birch branches
stretch out to us and wait and call,
and the powerful grandfather frosts march
in tight formation with us all.

[January 1942]

2.

In the starless January night,
astounded at the freak hand of fate,
back from death's abyss,
Leningrad salutes Leningrad.

[27 January 1944]

3.

Over the harbour a lighthouse flashed,
the signal for the other lighthouses.
The sailor took off his cap and wept.
He had sailed through the death-filled sea
past death to face death.

4.

Victory is standing at our door...
How will we greet the longed-for guest?
Let the women hold their children up high,
saved from a thousand thousand deaths,
this will be our answer to the one we've waited for so long.

[1942–1945]

17. *In Memory of a Friend*

And on Victory Day, tender, misty,
when the dawn glows red,
spring, late in coming, fusses,
like a widow by an unnamed grave.
She doesn't hurry to get off her knees, breathes
on an unopened leaf and strokes the grass,
and sets a butterfly from her shoulder onto the ground,
and puffs the first dandelion.

[1945]

'Anyone can do what I am doing'

The leper was praying...
V. Bryusov

Anyone can do what I am doing.
I did not drown in the Arctic sea, I did not die of thirst.

I did not take a strongpoint in Finland with a handful of brave
            men,
and did not save a ferry in the storm.

To go to bed, get up, eat a humble meal,
to sit on a rock by the road,

even to spot a shooting star,
or the familiar string of grey clouds,

to smile at them however strained the smile,
so I wonder all the more at my miraculous fate,

and although I get used to it, I can never quite get used to it,
as though it were a persistent, vigilant enemy.

[Fountain House, January 1941]

154

'Let us go now to Samarkand'

Let us go now to Samarkand,
to the immortal roses' homeland.

[1942]

From the Tashkent Notebook

Blessèd world and peace – green world and peace
at every turning.
Is this Baghdad or Cairo?
I fly like the bees to the honeycombs.
Is it Cairo or Baghdad?
No it is just an ordinary garden,
and a voice whispers 'Who's there?'
Those twigs brushed
the snow-white wall
with an elegance and simplicity
which does not exist in this world...

Death

I.

I was on the brink of something,
to which I cannot hang a name.
This half-sleep calling,
this slipping away from myself.

II.

I am already standing at the border of something
which comes to everyone at a different price.
There is a cabin for me on this ship,
and wind in the sails: the terrible moment
of parting with my own country.

[Dyurmen, 1942]

III.

If you are death, then why are you yourself crying?
If you are happiness, then this sort of happiness never happens.

IV. *Typhus*

Somewhere there's a young little night,
starry, frosty...
Oh my bad, bad
typhus head.

It imagines things about itself,
tosses on the pillow,
does not know, couldn't know,
that it must answer for everything,
that beyond the stream, beyond the garden
a nag is dragging a coffin.
I don't need to be buried,
I am the only story-teller.

[Tashkent, November 1942]

The Moon in the Zenith
Drafts of a Long Poem on Central Asia

Introduction

The whole sky is full of russet doves.
There are bars on the windows – the harem spirit...
A theme swells like a bud.
I cannot go back without you,
my fugitive, runaway poem.

But, perhaps, I will remember in flight
how Tashkent flared in flower,
enveloped in white flames,
hot, fragrant, premeditated,
improbable.

And so it was in that cursed year
when Madame Fifi was coarse
and brutal again as in the 1870s.
And I have to translate Lutfi
under the fire-breathing sunset.

The apple trees, forgive them God,
trembled like newly-weds.
The ditch mutters
in the local language – now allowed –
and I am finishing writing the poems of *Uneven*
in an anguish of composition.

I can see my poem clearly
up to the turning point – it's cool in it,
like in a house, where the darkness is fragrant,
and the windows are locked against the blazing heat,
where there is not a single hero yet,
but the poppy has flooded the roof with blood.

[Tashkent, Balakhan (attic), 8 November 1943]

1. 'To go to sleep worried'

To go to sleep worried,
to wake up in love,
to see the redness of the poppies.
Today a kind
of power has entered
into the sanctuary of darkness!
Brazier in the little courtyard,
how acrid your smoke is,
and how tall the poplar is.
Scheherazade walks
out of the garden:
so this is you then: the East!

[1942]

2. 'Was it you who sent me such coolness'

Was it you who sent me such coolness
from the menacing squares of Leningrad,
from the blessed Lethean fields.
Did you brighten up the hedgerows with poplars
and spread over my sadness
the myriad Asian stars?

3. 'Everything will come back to me again'

Everything will come back to me again,
the scorching night and the torment,
(as though Asia was delirious in its sleep)
the singing of Khalima, the nightingale songstress of Uzbekistan,
and the flowering of the Biblical narcissi –
an invisible blessing
rustles over the country in a breeze.

[1942]

4. 'And in the memory'

And in the memory, as though in patterned layers —
a smile, grown-grey, of all-knowing lips,
the noble folds of the graveyard turban
and the royal dwarf — the pomegranate bush.

[1944]

5. However much I am drawn'

However much I am drawn to golden-headed
                    Palmyra
nevertheless it is fated for me to live here
                    till the first rose.
The peach tree blossoms and the violets' mist
                    is black and violet...
Who will dare to say to me that this is
                    an evil foreign land?

6. 'I meet my third spring'

I meet my third spring far
                    from Leningrad.
The third? And it would seem it will
                    be my last.
The sound of water in the shade of the woods
                    was a joy to me
that I'll never forget till the day
                    I die.
The peach tree has blossomed and the violets' mist
                    wafts more fragrantly.
Who will dare to say to me that here
                    I'm in a foreign land?

7. 'Have I become someone completely different'

Have I become someone completely different
                from whom I was by the sea?
Have my lips forgotten
                the taste of grief?
I am at home again on this ancient,
                dry earth.
The Chinese wind sings in the haze
                and everything is familiar...
I hold my breath and look
                at the slopes.
I know that there are friends around,
                and millions of them.
The wind chases some sound on the wings
                of the night –
the heart of Asia beats
                and prophesies to me,
that I will again find asylum in
                the bright day of peace.
And somewhere near, just here, the fields
                of Kashmir are in flower.

8. 'You, Asia, homeland of homelands'

You, Asia, homeland of homelands!
The basin of mountains and deserts.
Your air is nothing like anything that ever existed,
it's so fiery and blue.
The neighbouring region appears
as an unprecedented fabled screen.
The flocks of pigeons over Burma
fly to indomitable China.
Great Asia kept quiet for a long time,
wrapped up in the flaming heat,
and concealed her eternal youth
under a menacing greyness.
But the bright era had approached
those forever sacred places
When you sang of Heser

160

everyone became characters in the Heseriad.
And you appeared before the world
with an olive branch in your hands
and a new truth sounded
in your ancient tongues.

9.   'I haven't been here for seven hundred years'

I haven't been here for seven hundred years,
but nothing has changed...
Still the same kindness of God flows
from the unequivocal skies,

still the same chorusses of stars and water,
still the same black skies,
and still the wind carries the grain,
and the mother sings the same song.

My Asian home is solid,
there's no need to be worried...
I'll come again. Flower hedgerows!
Let pure water fill the well.

10.   *The Moon Comes Out*
A.K.

Mother-of-pearl and agate,
through the smoked glass,
slanting so unexpectedly,
and so triumphantly it sailed forth
as though the 'Moonlight Sonata'
had suddenly cut across our path.

11. *'In the dining room'*

In the dining room – benches, table, window
with a huge silver moon.
We drink coffee and red wine,
we are delirious with the music…
                                        but it doesn't matter.
And the branch will blossom above the wall.
There was a sharp-edged sweetness in all of this,
an unrepeatable, yes, unrepeatable sweetness
of immortal roses and dried grapes.
The homeland had given us asylum.

[The whole cycle: Tashkent, 1942–1944]

'When the moon lies on the windowsill'

When the moon lies on the windowsill
like a slice of Asian melon, and everything is stifling,
when the door is shut and the house bewitched
by the featherlight, pale blue wisteria,
and there is cold water in the earthenware cup,
a snowy-white towel, and a wax candle
burns, attracting the moths, as it did in childhood –
everything is as though ready for the rites.
Only the silence thunders without cease not hearing my words.
Then from the terrible blackness of the Rembrandt corners,
something will whirl up suddenly and hide there again.
But I don't start. I'm not even afraid…
Here solitude has cast its net over me.
The landlady's black cat looks on with the eyes of centuries.
My double in the mirror does not want to help me.
I will sleep sweetly. Good night, night!

[Tashkent, 28 February 1944]

162

Tashkent Breaks into Blossom

1.

As if somebody ordered it
the city suddenly became bright —
every courtyard was visited
by white, light apparitions.
Their breathing is more understandable than words,
but their likeness is doomed to lie
at the bottom of the ditch
under the burning blue sky.

2.

I will remember the roof of stars
in the radiance of eternal glory,
and the little kids
in the young arms
of dark-haired mothers.

[1944]

'It was your lynx eyes, Asia'

It was your lynx eyes, Asia,
that spied something out in me,
teased out something hidden,
born of silence,
difficult and tormenting
like the midday heat at Termez.
As though all pre-memory flowed
into my conscience like red-hot lava.
As though I drank my own tears
from a stranger's cupped hands.

[1945]

F

Inscribed on the Poem

You came back to me famous,
wreathed with dark green twigs,
elegant, indifferent and proud...
You were different once
and not for this did I save
you then from the bloodbath.

I will not share success with you.
I do not triumph over you, but cry,
and you know perfectly well why.
The night goes on, I've not much strength left.
Save me, as I saved you,
and don't drop me into the seething darkness.

[Tashkent, 6 January 1944]

'I am what I am'

I am what I am — I wish you someone else —
someone better. I no longer deal in happiness,
like the charlatans and Bolsheviks do.
While you were peacefully resting in Sochi
what nights crept up on me,
what calls I received!
I did not listen to convict songs
as an important traveller resting in an armchair —
I learned them another way.

. . . .

The spring mists over Asia,
and tulips terrifyingly bright
carpeted many hundreds of miles.
What can I make of this purity
of nature and sacred innocence?

164

What can I make of these people?
I did not succeed in becoming just a spectator,
and for some reason always wedged myself
into the most forbidden zones of human nature –
the healer of the tender sickness,
the most faithful friend of others' husbands,
the inconsolable widow of many.

Not in vain is the crown of grey mine.
My face is so sunburned
it frightens people.
But pride comes before a fall:
like that other martyr Marina,
I have to drink emptiness to the dregs.

You will come to me in a black cloak,
holding a greenish, terrifying candle
and will not show me your face.
But I don't have to torture myself with the riddle for long:
whose hand is it under the white glove
and who sent the night visitor?

[Tashkent, 24 June 1942]

'You like to call to the tomtit'

You like to call to the tomtit
that nests under the floorboards
and somehow enter the dreams
of those who groan in their sleep beside you,
but will not breathe a word
even to their friend.

[1942]

'The double hides his Bourbon profile'

The double hides his Bourbon profile in the mirror
and thinks that he is indispensable,
that he will turn the world upside down,
that he will outpasternak Pasternak,
and I don't know what to do with him.

[Tashkent, 1943]

'I would not have seen the quince flower bloom'
To In. Busudaev as a memory of our Tashkent

I would not have seen the quince flower bloom,
would not have known how words sound
in your language,
how the mist crawls down the mountains into the town
and how the caravan passes
through dusty Beshaghach square,
like a ray of sun, like a wind, like a torrent.

      *   *

This town is ancient as the earth itself,
and is moulded from pure clay.
The boundless fields
overflow with tulips.

      *   *

I thank you all now:
I say Rahmat and Khair
and wave my kerchief.

Rahmat, Aibek, rahmat, Chusti,
rahmat Toshkent! – Farewell, farewell,
my quiet, ancient home.
Rahmat to the stars and the flowers
and the little kids in the young arms
of dark-haired mothers.
For eight hundred magical days
I breathed in the burning garden
under your blue cup,
your lapis lazuli chalice.

[Leningrad, 28 September 1945]

Beshaghach: 'Five trees' in Turkish.
Rahmat: 'thanks', Khair: 'farewell' in Uzbek.
Aibek and *Chusti:* Uzbek writers.

From the Plane

I.

Over thousands of *versts*, over thousands of miles,
over thousands of kilometres,
salt lay, grass rustled,
the cedar groves loomed.
As though for the first time in my whole life
I was looking at my homeland,
I realised it's all mine –
my body, and my soul.

II.

I will mark that day with a white stone,
when, outstripping the sun, I flew
to meet victory head on
and sang of the victory I knew.

III.

The grass of the spring
aerodrome rustles underfoot.
Home, real homecoming!
How new yet familiar everything is
and how good the heart feels!
and the head spins sweetly
in the fresh May thunder.
Moscow the Victorious!

[May 1944]

Lament

I will not brush aside
the Leningrad disaster.
I will not wash it away with tears,
I will not bury it in the earth.
I will avoid the Leningrad
disaster from a distance.
But I'll remember it in my prayers,
not with a look, nor a hint,
nor a word, nor a reproach,
but with a bow to the earth
     in the green field.

[Leningrad, 1944]

Liberated

The clean wind lulls the fir trees,
the clean snow sweeps the fields.
My land is at rest,
and no longer hears the tramp of enemy boots.

[1945]

168

'Distant delineations of Faust'

Distant delineations of Faust,
like cities, where there are many black towers
and clocktowers with resonant clocks,
and stormy midnights,
and little old men with ungoethean fates,
organ grinders, moneychangers and booksellers,
who called up the devil, who traded with him
and deceived him and left us this bargain
in their will...
The deadly trumpets blared,
the violins were reverent in the face of death,
when some strange instrument
gave a warning and a woman's voice
responded – and then I woke up.

[1945]

'He, whom the people mockingly called King'

He, whom the people mockingly called King,
but who was in fact God,
who was killed and whose instrument of torture
is warmed by the heat of my breast...

Christ's witnesses tasted death,
the old gossips, the soldiers,
the Roman proconsul – they have all gone.
Where once the arch was raised on high,
where the sea beats on the black cliffs –
they drank to them in the wine, breathed them in the hot dust
and the scent of blessèd roses.

Gold rusts and steel decays,
marble gets crushed – everything is ready for death.
Sadness is the most constant thing on earth,
and the royal word is even more eternal.

[1945(?)]

'With the lads in the gutter'

With the lads in the gutter
by the pub,
with the prisoners on the bench
in the lorry,

in the thick mist
over the Moscow river,
with the robber chief
in the taut noose:

I was with them all,
with these and with those,
but now I am left –
with myself.

[Fountain House, 1946]

'One takes the straight line'

One takes the straight line,
another goes in a circle
and longs for the return to the parents' house
and longs for a former girlfriend.
But I go, not in a straight line or in a zigzag,
into nowhere and never,
and disasters follow me
like trains crashing off the tracks.

[1940]

Youth

My young hand signed
that agreement among the flower stalls
and the rasping gramophones,
under the squint, drunk eye
of the street gaslights.
And I was ten years
older than the century.

The white mourning clothes of the cherry blossom
were laid against the sunset
to scatter a fine
fragrant, dry rain...
The clouds were shot through
with a bloody Tsushima foam,
and the carriages rolled along smoothly
carrying those who are now dead.

The evenings in those days
seemed to us to be a masquerade,
seemed to be a carnival,
a *grand-gala* fairy-tale ballet.

Not a splinter of wood is left over from my old house,
and they have chopped down the avenue of trees,
and the hats and shoes of those days
have long ago been laid to rest in the museum.
And who knows how empty
the sky is where the tower fell?
Who knows how silent it is in the home
to which the son did not return?
You are as persistent as conscience,
always over me like the sky above.
Why do you call me to account?
I know your witnesses:
the dome of the Pavlovsk station,
incandescent with music,
and the white-maned waterfall
by the Babolov palace.

[1940]

Smolensk Graveyard

You were all I ever found on this earth:
last century's withered harvest.
. . . .
Everything was ending here: dinner at Donon's,
intrigues and ranks, ballet, expense accounts...
A noble crown on an ancient pedestal,
and a little rusty angel cries dry tears.
The East was still an unknown expanse
and roared in the distance like a menacing enemy camp,
and the West wafted over a Victorian arrogance,
a shower of confetti and the howling of the can-can.

[Dyurmen, 1942]

Hearthwarming
(to E.S. Bulgakova)

1. *Mistress of the House*

In this room there lived
a witch, before I moved in.
Her shadow can still be seen
on the eve of the new moon.
Her shadow still stands
by the high threshold,
and looks at me
evasively and sternly.
I myself am not one of those
who is under the power of others' spells.
I myself...However, I will not
give away my secrets for nothing.

[1943]

2. *Guests*

       '...You are drunk,
all the same it's time to get back home...'
Don Juan grown old
and Faust grown young again
bumped into each other by my gate –
after the tavern and their *rendezvous*.
Or was this only the twigs brushing
under a black wind,
with the green magic of beams,
transfused as though with poison?
And yet – they are like two people I know,
so alike that I feel revulsion.

[1943]

3. *Treachery*

Not because the mirror shattered,
not because the wind whined in the chimney,
not because in thinking of you
something else filtered into my mind:
that was definitely not the reason why
I met him on the threshold.

[1944]

4. *Meeting*

Almost like the happy little refrain
of a terrible little song –
he comes up the shaky staircase
            and our parting is over.
Not I to him, but he to me –
and doves at the window...
And the courtyard in ivy, and you're wearing your coat,
            as I used to tell you to.
Not he to me, but I to him,
            in the darkness,
                        in the darkness,
                                    in the darkness.

[Tashkent, 1943]

Three Autumns

For me summer smiles indistinctly,
I find no secrets in winter,
but I could pick out unerringly
three autumns in each year.

The first a holiday chaos
spiting yesterday's summer.

176

Leaves fly like notebook scraps,
smoke smells sweet as incense,
everything moist, gay and bright.

First the birches start the dance
throwing on their transparent attire,
hastily shaking off their fleeting tears
on their neighbour over the fence.

This is what happens...the tale is scarce begun...
a second, a minute – and look,
the second one comes, passionless like conscience,
sombre as an air raid.

Everything suddenly seems paler, older.
Summer's comfort is plundered,
marches in the distance played on golden trumpets
float over the scented fog...

The lofty sky is concealed
in cold waves of incense,
but the wind started blowing,
all was swept open, and immediately
everyone understood: the play is ending,
this is not the third autumn – but death.

[1943]

Near Kolomna
(for the Shervinskys)

...Where the bell-tower rises
like a cat arching to spring,
where there is a smell of mint in the fields,
and the poppies stroll around in red bonnets
and the Moscow river flows –
everything is made of timber, crafted from wood.
The minute filters its every grain
in the hour glass. This garden

is denser than all gardens and forests,
and above it, as over a bottomless abyss,
the ancient sun looks intently,
tenderly, from a blue-grey cloud.

[1943]

'All the souls of the dear ones'

All the souls of the dear ones are among the stars.
How good it is that there is no one to lose
and tears can just flow. The air at Tsarskoye Selo
was created to repeat songs.

The silver willow touches
the bright September waters by the shore.
My shadow comes towards me,
silently resurrected from the past.

So many lyres hang on the branches here,
but there would appear to be a place for mine too.
And this fine, sunny shower,
comforts me, and brings good tidings.

[1921]

'Everyone went away'

> *The waste land of the numb squares*
> *where they executed the people before dawn.*
> Innokenty Annensky

Everyone went away and no one came back,
but, true to your promise of love,
my last one, you alone looked back
to see the whole sky in blood.

178

The house was damned, the cause was damned.
In vain the song rang out more tenderly
and I didn't dare raise my eyes
before my terrible fate.
They sullied the most pure word,
trampled the holy language,
so that I should scrub the bloodstained
floor with the sick-nurses of '37.
They parted me with my only son,
tortured my friends in the solitary cells.
They surrounded me with an invisible
stockade of round-the-clock shadowing.
They rewarded me with dumbness,
cursed and damned the whole world.
They force-fed me with slander,
forced me to drink poison
and taking me to the very edge
for some reason left me there –
I will wander the silenced
squares like the city madwoman.

[Late 1940s]

The Last Return

> *I have one road, one single road:*
> *from the window to the threshold.*
> Song

Day followed after day, this and that
happened almost as usual,
but loneliness permeated
through it all.
Smell of tobacco,
mice, an opened chest,
and a small cloud of poison
mist clustered in the air.

[1944]

'The man who means nothing to me now'

...The man who means nothing to me now,
but was my worry
and comfort through the bitterest years,
wanders deliriously like a ghost
around the outskirts, the back alleys
and backyards of my life,
heavy, drugged with madness
with a wolfish grin...
         My God! My God! My God!
How horribly I sinned before Thee!
Just leave me compassion.

[1945]

'I do not have any special claim'

I do not have any special claim
on this illustrious house,
but it so happened that I lived
almost all my life under the famous roof
of the Fountain Palace...A beggar I entered it
and a beggar I will leave it.

[1952]

'Others take their loved ones with them'

Others take their loved ones with them –
I feel jealous and cannot watch.
I have been sitting on the trial bench
for almost half a century.

180

Bureaucracy and crowds of people,
and the sickly sweet smell of ink.
Kafka thought up this sort of thing,
and Charlie Chaplin portrayed it.
And after those important wrangles
as in the tenacious embraces of nightmare,
all three generations of jurors
decided: she is guilty.
The faces of the guards keep changing,
the sixth public prosecutor has a heart attack.
Somewhere the huge expanse of the heavens
looms dark in the heat,
and summer, full of charms,
strolls on the opposite shore.
But I cannot imagine
that blessed "somewhere".
I have gone deaf from the volume of curses.
I have worn out my quilted jacket.
Was I really the most
guilty person on this planet?

[Mid–1950s]

'It is no wonder that my unruly poems'

It is no wonder that my unruly poems
sound unhappy and that I myself am sad.
Three quarters of my readers
are already beyond the Phlegethon.

As for you few remaining friends
you are dearer to me every day.
How short the road became
that had seemed to be so long.

[1958]

'In vain you cast at my feet'

I see my swan is at play
Pushkin

In vain you cast at my feet
greatness, fame and power.
You know very well you cannot get rid
of the bright passion of poetry.
You cannot make good the insult and injury like that:
sadness cannot be cured with gold.
Perhaps for the sake of appearances I'll yield.
I won't put the pistol to my head.
Death is at the doorstep,
chase it away or call it in,
and behind it stretches the dark road
up which I crawled in blood.
Behind it: decades
of boredom, fear and that emptiness
which I could write poems about,
but I fear that you'd pay for them.
Farewell then! I don't live in a waste land,
I have the night and eternal old Russia.
Just save me from pride!
The rest I can manage.

[Moscow, 1957(?)]

'They will forget'

They will forget! You surprise me!
They've forgotten me hundreds of times.
A hundred times I have lain in the grave,
where I am perhaps right now.
And the Muse went deaf and blind,

182

and rotted like a seed in the earth,
so as later like a Phoenix from the ashes
to rise again into the blue ether.

[Leningrad, 21 February 1957]

'So I have no flight out'

So I have no flight out
of the flock of swans...
O dear! The lyric poet
has to be a man,
or else everything will be upside down
before the hour of parting –
and the garden won't be a garden, the house not a house,
and the meeting – not a meeting.

Inscribed in a Book

What you've given away is yours
Shota Rustaveli

From under what rubble do I speak,
from under what avalanche do I scream –
I burn as in quicklime
under the vaults of the stinking cellar.
I will pretend to be a silent winter,
and slam the doors of eternity forever,
but they will recognise my voice nevertheless,
and trust in it again, despite everything.

[Leningrad, 13 January 1959]

Heiress

From the limes of Sarskoye Selo...
Pushkin

It seemed to me that a song was sung
among these deserted halls.
Who would have said to me then
that I would inherit all this:
Felitsa, the swan, the bridges
and the Chinese pavilions,
the spacious galleries of the palace
and the wondrously beautiful limes;
and even my own shadow,
disfigured with fear,
and the penitent's shirt,
and lilac on the grave.

[1959]

'What does parting mean to us'

What does parting mean to us
if not wicked amusement?
Disasters grow bored without us.
Will fame drop drunkenly into the chamber?
Will the thirteenth hour strike?
Or in oblivion, obliterated, ob...
knocked out, nothing, kno...Who's
learnt to knock at the door like that?
I must go back to the gates again
to meet a new grief.

[1959]

184

To the Poem

...let the word return to music
O. Mandelstam

You flower and grow, you are in the sound.
I resurrected you to be tortured again
and handed you over to the enemy.
Eight thousand miles is no barrier,
it's as though the song is outside in the garden,
I can even check its breathing.
I know the same thing is happening to him,
and I cannot reproach him:
this union is beyond our control.
Both of us are not guilty on all counts.
Our sacrifices were bloodless –
I forgot, and he – forgot.

[Komarovo, 20 September 1960]

Prologue

I don't come with a lover's lyre
to captivate the people.
My poems are like
the leper's rattle.
You will have time to groan
and howl and curse.
I will teach you, 'the bold ones',
to shy away from me.
I did not seek gain,
or fame or praise:
for thirty long years I lived
under destruction's wing.

A String of Quatrains

Never mind wars and plagues. They'll be over soon;
their sentence has almost been pronounced.
But how can we live with this terror
which was once called 'the flight of time'?

*

To be honest
for this clowning minstrelsy
I should expect a lead
pellet from the secretary.

[1937]

The Lord, crucified on every tree,
the body of Christ in every ear of corn,
and the purest word of prayer
heal the aching flesh.

To Poetry

You led us to where we could not get
like a shooting star into the darkness.
You were lies and bitterness
but never – comfort.

The Death of the Demon

The moon beam traced that profile
as though it were Vrubel inspired.
And the blessèd wind disclosed
Lermontov's secrets.

*

When I drank in the burning heat
my heart needed nothing.
Eugene Onegin's atmospheric mass
hung over me like a storm cloud.

*

Glances fiercer than fire.
The pagan God Lel's smile.
Don't deceive me —
April fool!

*

Thoughts, feelings disappear
in this breeze.
Today even the luggage of eternal art
is that little bit lighter!

My Name:

Tatar, dense textured,
came from nowhere,
sticks to any disaster,
in fact it is disaster!

*

Fame swam out like a swan
through the golden mist,
and you, love, were always
my despair.

*

No longer will I mourn my fate,
but I never want to see in this life
the golden brand of failure
on his still untroubled brow.

[1962]

Second Anniversary

No, I didn't cry them out:
tears only boiled up inside me,
and everything passes before my eyes
without them for so long, always without them.

Without them the pain of injury, of parting,
torments me, suffocates me.
Their all-consuming salt fire
seeped into the blood, sobers up and dries out.

But I remember your shadow
of suffering, as it was on my homecoming
on first June 1944,
as though cast on worn silk cloth.

The impression was still raw, still fresh
of the great disasters, the recent storms,
and I saw my town again
through a rainbow of last tears.

[Leningrad, 1 June 1946]

Inscribed on a Portrait
(to T.V.)

The smoky offspring of the full moon,
white marble in the twilight avenues,
fateful girl, dancer,
the best of all the cameos.
People died as a result of such women.
Genghis Khan sent his envoy for such a one,
and one of them carried the head of the Baptist
on a bloodstained platter.

[1946]

188

Cinque

Autant que toi sans doute, il te sera fidèle,
Et constant jusques à la mort.
Baudelaire

1.

The memory of your words
is like being on the edge of a cloud,

and my words made your
nights brighter than your days.

And so, wrenched from the earth,
we moved through space like stars.

Neither despair, nor shame,
not now, not after, not then.

In the reality of everyday
you hear me calling you.

I have no strength to slam
the door you opened just a little.

[26 November 1945]

2.

Sounds smoulder to ashes in the air,
and the dawn pretended to be darkness.
Just two voices: yours and mine
in the eternally numbed world,
And under the wind from the invisible Ladoga lakes,
through a sound like the ringing of bells,
the night's conversation was turned
into the light sparkle of crossed rainbows.

[20 December 1945]

3.

I have never liked people to pity me,
even from days long ago,
but I go on with a drop of your pity
as though I carry the sun within me.
That's why the dawn is all around.
That's why I go on working miracles.

[20 December 1945]

4.

You know yourself that I will not begin to celebrate
that most bitter day of our meeting.
What can I leave you as a memory,
my shadow? What do you want with my shadow?
The dedication of a burnt drama,
from which there is no ash?
Or a terrifying New Year's portrait
suddenly coming out of the frame?
Or the whisper of birch embers
barely, barely heard?
Or that they failed
to convince me of a stranger's love?

[6 January 1946]

5.

We didn't breathe in soporific poppies,
and we do not know of what we are guilty.
Under just what star signs
were we born to bring each other grief?

What Hell's brew did
this January darkness bring?
And what unseen luminous delight
drove us out of our minds before dawn?

[11 January 1946]

190

The Sweetbriar in Bloom

From a Burnt Notebook

And thou art distant in humanity
Keats

Instead of festive greetings
this hard, dry wind,
will bring you the smell of burning,
the taste of smoke and poems
which I had written by hand.

[24 December 1961]

1. *Burnt Notebook*

Now your accomplished sister
adorns the book shelf,
but over you are the shivers of flocks of stars,
and under you are the coals of the fire.
How you prayed, how you wanted to live,
how you feared the caustic flames!
But suddenly your body flickered
and as your voice flew off it cursed me.
All the pines started rustling then,
and were reflected in the depths of the moon waters.
The rites of spring were danced
around the fiery grave.

[1961]

2. *In Reality*

Away with time, away with space,
I saw everything through the white night:
the narcissus in the crystal vase on the table at your house,
and the blue cigar smoke,

191

and that mirror where I might see
your reflection, as in clear water.
Away with time, away with space...
but even you cannot help me.

[13 June 1946]

3. *In a Dream*

As an equal, I bear with you
our black permanent separation.
Are you crying? Just give me your hand:
and promise to come again in a dream.
You and I are mountains facing each other.
You and I will never meet on this earth.
If only you could send me at midnight
a greeting through the stars.

[1946]

4. *First Song*

The celebrations of the secret
non-meeting are empty.
Unspoken speech,
unpronounced words.
Uncrossed glances
do not know where to land,
and only tears are happy
because they can flow for a long time.
Yes, I'm afraid the sweetbriar
of the Moscow countryside
has something to do with it...
And all this they call
immortal love.

5. Another Song

I will no longer repeat
unspoken words.
But in memory of that non-meeting
I will plant a sweetbriar.

There the miracle of our meeting
shone and sang,
I did not want to go back
to anywhere from there.
Putting happiness before duty
was my bitter joy.

I talked with someone I shouldn't have.
I talked for a long time.
Let passions which demand an answer
choke those who are in love,
but we, my darling, are just souls
at the edge of the earth.

[1956]

6. A Dream

Is it sweet to see other-worldly dreams?
Alexander Blok

The dream might have been a prophecy...
Mars shone bright among the stars in the sky,
it became crimson giving off malevolent sparks,
and that night I dreamed of your arrival.

He was in everything...In the Bach chaconne,
in the roses that bloomed in vain,
and in the ringing of the village bell
above the blackness of the ploughed fields.

And in the autumn that approached in earnest,
suddenly thought and hid itself again.
O my August, how could you give
such news on this terrible Anniversary!

How shall I pay back this royal present?
Where shall I go and with whom shall I celebrate?
And now I write my poems in the burnt notebook
without corrections as before.

[Near Kolomna, 14 August 1956]

7.

Along that road
where Donskoy once led his great army,
where the wind remembers the enemy,
where the moon is a yellow, horned crescent,
where I walked, as though in the depth of the sea...
The sweetbriar was so fragrant
that it became the word
and I was ready to meet
the seventh wave of my fate.

8.

You invented me. There is no such person,
there could be no such person on earth.
The doctor cannot cure, nor the poet soothe you,
from that apparition that troubles you, day and night.
You and I met in an improbable year,
when the powers of the world had already dried up,
everything was in mourning, everything wilted from suffering,
and only the graves were fresh.
The Neva embankment was black as pitch without streetlamps.
The dense night encircled the wall...
So it was then my voice sent for you.
What I did I could not understand myself.
You came to me as though guided by a star,
walking in the tragic autumn,
into the house ruined for ever,
from where the flock of burnt poems flew away.

[18 August 1956]

9. *In a Broken Mirror*

On that starry evening
I listened to words that could not be taken back
and my head began to spin
as though I was over a flaming chasm.
Death howled at the doors.
The black garden hooted like a screech owl,
and the city, in its mortal weakness,
was more ancient than Troy.
The unbearably clear hour
rang until tears fell.
Instead of the present, which you had brought
from afar, you gave me something else:
what seemed to be just an amusing conversation
in an intense evening for you,
became the slow poison
in my enigmatic fate.
It was the precursor of all my troubles –
let us not remember it!
The meeting that never took place
still weeps behind the corner.

[1956]

10.

> *You are with me again, my friend autumn!*
> Innokenty Annensky

They may still be resting in the South
and basking in the heavenly garden,
but it's very northern here, and this year
I picked autumn for a friend.

I live in a strange house that I once dreamed of,
and where perhaps I died,
and it seems Finland takes secret looks
into the empty mirrors.

I walk through the black forest of dwarf firs,
where the heather is like wind,
and the dull fragment of moon shines
like a jagged old knife.

I brought here the blessed memory
of my last non-meeting with you –
the cold, clear, light flame
of my victory over fate.

[Komarovo, 1956]

11.

*It was not by my own will, your Majesty, that I departed
from your shores...*
                    Aeneid 6

Don't be afraid – I can still vividly
picture us as we were.
Are you a ghost, or a man passing through?
For some reason I preserve your shadow.

You were not my Aeneas for long.
The funeral pyre was my escape.
We know how to be silent about each other.
And you forgot my cursed house.

You forgot the hands that stretched
through the fire in terror and suffering,
and the news of a hope that was damned.

You don't know for what you were forgiven...
Rome is founded, the flotillas sail
and flattery eulogises the victory.

[Komarovo, 1962]

12.

You insist on having my poems...
You'll live somehow – even without them.
There is not a drop of my blood
that has not absorbed their bitterness.

We burn up the splendid, golden days
of this impossible life,
and the night lights do not include us
in their whispers of a meeting in the fatherland of heaven.

A cold chill emanates
from our deeds,
as if we trembled reading out
names at a mysterious crypt.

It would have been better to part immediately.
Now we cannot imagine anything
in this world more endless
than this parting of ours.

[Moscow 1963]

13.

The cunning moon
hiding by the gates saw how
I exchanged my posthumous fame
for that evening.
Now they will forget me,
my books will rot in the cupboard.
They will call
no street or stanza Akhmatova.

[1946]

14.

The people will regard this time
as the age of Vespasian,
but it was really only a wound
with a little cloud of suffering over it.

[Rome, night, 18 December 1964]

From the *Burnt Notebook Cycle*

Even if my ship has sunk,
and the house has gone up in smoke...
You can all read this, I don't mind.
I am talking to one man
who was not guilty of anything,
and who, incidentally, is a stranger:
neither my fiancé nor my brother.
. . . .
How does it feel to be stabbed in the heart
and hear the shout 'Die!'
What poem did the lamps write
in gold on the Fontanka?

[1956]

Midnight Verses
Seven Poems

Only mirror dreams of mirror,
silence guards silence...
Tails

Introduction

If the glass which once
clinked as it was swept up,
joined together again –
this is what would have survived.

In Place of a Dedication

I roam the waves and hide in the forest,
I appear on the sky's pure enamel.
Parting I will probably take quite well,
but a meeting with you, hardly.

[Summer 1963]

1. Elegy before the Coming of Spring

...toi qui m'a consolée
Gérard de Nerval

The snowstorm grew quiet among the pines,
silence itself, drunk even without wine,
sang like Ophelia,
to us throughout the night.
He who appeared only to me
was betrothed to that silence.
After he'd said goodbye he generously remained,
he remained with me till death.

[Komarovo, 10 March 1963]

199

2. First Forewarning

In fact what business of ours is it
that everything turns to dust and ashes?
I have sung over so many chasms,
I have lived in so many mirrors.
I may not be a dream, nor joy
and least of all a blessing,
but perhaps more often than necessary
you will remember
the hum of lines that grew still,
and the rusty, barbed wreath
that I see in my mind's eye
in its troubled silence.

[Moscow, 6 July 1963]

3. Through the Looking Glass

> O quae beatam Diva, tenes Cyprum et Memphin...
>   Horace

We cannot be just the two of us.
That third will never leave us:
a very young beauty
of another century.
You will move the chair close to her,
I share the flowers with her...
We ourselves don't know what we are doing,
but every moment becomes more terrifying.
As though we have come out of prison
each knowing something terrible about the other.
We are in the circle of hell,
but perhaps it isn't even us.

[Komarovo, 5 July 1963]

4. Thirteen Lines

Finally you spoke the word,
not like a proposal –
but like someone who's escaped from prison
and sees through a rainbow of involuntary tears
the sacred canopy of birches.
Silence sang out around you
and the twilight was illuminated by pure sun.
The world was transformed for one moment,
and the wine tasted strange.
Even I, whose destiny it was
to murder the eternal word,
fell silent almost reverently
and therefore was able to carry on living this blessèd life.

[Komarovo, 8–12 August 1963]

5. The Call
Arioso Dolente: Beethoven's penultimate Sonata

I hide you cautiously
in one of the sonatas.
Oh, what fear there is in your voice,
irreversibly guilty
for having approached me,
even though for just one moment...
Your dream is to disappear
where death is only a sacrifice
to that familiar silence.

[1 July 1963]

6. The Visit at Night
Everyone has gone away and no one has returned.

You won't wait for long on the pavement
      where the leaves fall.
You and I will meet again in
      Vivaldi's Adagio.

Again the candles will be dim and fade,
    bewitched by sleep.
The violin will not question
    how you came into my midnight house.
These half hours will flow by
    in a silent, deathly lament.
you will read on the palm of my hand
    the same miracles.
Then your fear will
    become your fate
and carry you away from my threshold
    on an icy wave.

[Komarovo, 10–13 September 1963]

7.   And Last

It was over us, like a star over the sea,
searching with its beam for the deadly seventh wave.
You called it disaster and grief,
and never once called it joy.

By day it circled us like a swallow,
blossomed like a smile on the lips,
But at night, in different cities
it choked us both with an icy hand

Heedless to any eulogies,
oblivious of all former sins,
it comes to the bedsides of the most sleepless
and whispers the cursed poems.

[23–25 June 1963]

Instead of an Afterword

Where they create dreams,
there were not enough for both of us,
so we saw the same one, but there was a power
in that dream, like the coming of spring.

[1965]

202

Moscow Trefoil

Almost in an Album

You will hear thunder and remember me
and think – she wanted storms.
The horizon will be hard crimson
and the heart will burn as before.

That's how it will be on that Moscow day,
when I leave the city for ever
and rush to where I long for,
still leaving my shadow among you.

Untitled

Over frosty, festive Moscow
where our parting is now happening
and where you will probably read
the first edition of these farewell poems,
the eyes stare in surprise...
'What? What? Already? It's not possible!'
                                    Of course!
The turquoise of the Christmas sky,
everything around is blessèd, sinless.
There has never ever been a parting like ours –
and this is the reward
              for our endeavour.

One More Toast

To your faith! And to my faithfulness!
To the fact that we are together in this land.
Perhaps we will be under a spell eternally,
but there was nothing finer than that winter,
nothing more finely patterned than the crosses in the sky,
nothing more airy than the little chains on the embankment,
nothing longer than the bridges...

To the fact that everything flowed, silently sliding.
To the fact that we are not allowed to see each other.
To what I see in my dreams even now –
though the door that led there is now solidly boarded up.

[1961–1963]

'That fruit-bearing autumn'

Here it is that fruit-bearing autumn –
she has come rather late.
I didn't dare rise from the ground
for fifteen most blessed springs.
I looked her over closely,
fell at her feet, embraced her,
and the autumn poured her secret power
secretly into my doomed body.

[13 September 1962]

On Not Sending the Poem

Wind gusts by the sea.
A home in which we do not live
and the shade of the most cherished cedar
outside the most forbidden window...
There is someone in this world to whom I could
send all these poems. So what?
Let lips smile bitterly,
and my heart shudder again.

[1963]

Uneven

Sonnet by the Sea

Here everything will outlive me,
everything, even these dilapidated starling boxes,
and this air, this spring air
that has flown over the sea.

The voice of eternity calls
invincibly, unearthly.
Over the blossoming cherry tree
the light moon pours radiance.

this road, leading I will not say where,
seems so uncomplicated,
as it gleams white in the emerald thicket.

There it is even brighter among the trunks
and ever more like the alley
by the pond in Tsarskoye Selo.

[Komarovo, 1958]

Music
D.D. Shostakovich

It creates miracles.
In its eyes limits are defined.
It alone talks with me
when others are afraid to come near,
when the last friend has turned his eyes away.
It was with me in my grave
and sang like the first storm,
or as though all the flowers had burst into speech.

[1958]

206

Drawing in a Book of Poems

The frail black and white garland
of a half-abandoned bride
is neither funeral nor sombre –
almost like translucent smoke.
That aquiline profile,
and the satin of the Paris fringe,
and the green, oblong,
very vigilant eyes.

[1958]

Fragment

...And it seemed that these were fires
flying with me until dawn,
and I did not learn
what colour these strange eyes were.

And everything around trembled and sang,
and I did not find out if you were friend or foe,
if this was winter or summer.

[1959]

Summer Garden

I want to go to the roses, to that unique garden,
where the railings are the finest in the world,

where the statues remember me when I was young –
I remember them under the waters of the Neva.

In the fragrant silence among the royal limes
I seem to hear the creak of ships' masts.

The swan, as before, floats through the ages
admiring the beauty of its double,

and hundreds of thousands of footsteps of enemies and friends,
of friends and enemies sleep the sleep of the dead.

The procession of shadows never ends
from the granite vase to the palace gates.

There my white nights whisper
of someone's lofty, secret love,

and everything burns in mother-of-pearl and jasper,
but the source of the light is mysteriously concealed.

[July 1959]

'Don't frighten me'

Don't frighten me with threats of fate
and the vast boredom of the North without you.
This is my first holiday with you,
they call this holiday – parting.
Never mind that we did not greet the dawn,
that the moon did not roam above us,
today I will give you
gifts unheard of in this world:
my reflection in the water
in the hour when the evening stream is sleepless,
the look that did not help
the shooting star to return to the heavens.
The echo of a tired, faint voice
which once was fresh and summery –
so that you could hear without shuddering
the gossip of the crows round Moscow,

so that the damp of an October day
became sweeter than the softness of May.
Remember me, my angel,
remember me, at least till the first snow.

[Yaroslav Highway, 15 October 1959]

To Pushkin's Town

And the sheltering halls of Sarskoye Selo
Pushkin

1.

Oh God! They've burnt you down...
This meeting is harder to bear than parting!
Here was the fountain, the lofty avenues,
the broad mass of the ancient park in the distance.
The sunset was more crimson than itself.
There was a smell of compost and earth in April;
and my first kiss...

[1944]

2.

The leaves of this willow tree faded in the 19th century,
to be silvered afresh a hundredfold in a line of poetry.
The rose turned wild and became a purple sweetbriar,
and the Lycée hymns still ring out to your health.
Half a century has passed...generously restored by a miraculous
        fate.
I forgot the years' flow in the oblivion of days,
I cannot go back there. But I shall take across the Lethe itself
the living outlines of my Tsarskoye Selo gardens.

[1957]

3.

They have burnt down my toy town,
and I no longer have a loophole to the past.
The fountain was there, the green benches,
and the mass of the Royal park in the distance.
Pancakes at Shrovetide; and Finnish cab drivers avoiding the
        pot-holes.
There was a smell of compost and earth in April;
and my first kiss.

[1946]

Little Songs

1. *Song of the Road or a Voice from the Darkness*

If you are afraid of something,
then it will happen.
You mustn't be afraid of anything.
This song has been sung,
but that one hasn't,
and that other one
is also like it.
      Oh Lord!

[1943]

2. *Superfluous Song*

Terror comforted, snowstorms warmed.
Darkness took us through the valley of death.
We are wrenched apart from each other...
This cannot be.
If you want I'll cast off the spell,
let me try to be good.
Choose anything –
but not this agony.

[1959]

3. *Farewell Song*

I didn't laugh, I didn't write poems,
but was silent for the whole day.
I had wanted it all with you
from the very beginning;
the first carefree argument
full of bright deliriums,
and the rough, hasty,
last shared meal, when we didn't speak.

[1959]

4. *Love Song*

We did not
    share love,
but we shared
    everything then.
For you – the white light of the world,
    free roads,
for you – dawns
    with bells ringing.
But for me – wadding boots,
    a cap with ear flaps.
Do not pity me,
    the little convict woman.

5. *Drinking Song*

One cannot see the work table
under a patterned tablecloth.
I was not mother to my poems
but stepmother.
Oh, the white paper,
the even rows of lines!
How many times did I watch them burn.
Mutilated by slander,
lashed by the whip,

branded, branded
with the convict's brand.

[1955]

6. Last One

I used to delight in delirium
and singing of the grave.
I used to bring about disasters
that transcend all powers.
The curtain was not yet raised
on the round dance of shadows,
that's why the one who was taken
from me was my dearest.
I disclose this
to the very depth of roses.
But I am not allowed to
forget the taste of yesterday's tears.

[1964]

From The Cycle of Tashkent Pages

That night we had driven each other mad,
only an ominous darkness lit our way,
the ditches muttered,
carnations smelt of Asia.

We passed through a strange town,
through a smoky song and midnight heat;
alone under the constellation of the Snake
not daring to look at each other.

This could be Baghdad or Stamboul
but alas, not Warsaw or Leningrad,
and this bitter anomaly was
suffocating like the smell of an orphanage.

212

It seemed ages marched beside us,
an invisible hand beat a tambourine.
Sounds like secret signs
circled before us in the dark.

I was with you in the mysterious haze
as though we were walking in no-man's-land,
but the moon like a diamond felucca
suddenly sailed out over our meeting-parting...

And if that night comes back to you,
in the course of your fate which is a mystery to me,
know that this sacred moment
was somebody's dream.

[1959]

'You live on, but I won't live long'

You live on, but I won't live long,
that turning point is near.
O, how severe and precise
is the Invisible's account.

Wild animals are shot at different times,
each has its turn
in a variety of ways,
but it's open season for the wolf.

The wolf likes to live in freedom,
but his account is swiftly settled:
on the ice, in the forest, in the field,
they shoot him the whole year round.

Don't cry, my only friend,
in summer or winter
you'll hear my cry
from the wolf path.

[20 November–2 December 1959]

'Distance collapsed in rubble'

Distance collapsed in rubble and time shook
and accelerated and diabolically stamped on the brows
of great mountains and reversed the river's flow.
The seed lay poisoned in the earth,
the sap flowed poisoned in the stem.
A whole generation of people died,
but everyone knew that the time was very near.

[1950s]

'There's a voice outside the door'

There's a voice outside the door:
someone is calling out our names,
and in answer something flashed
in the dark corner in the murky mirror
and plunged a golden needle
into my heart, as a joke.

March Elegy

Last year's treasures, I fear,
will last me a long time.
You know yourself evil memory
can in no way spend the half of them:
the dome smashed on its side,
the cawing of the crows,
the piercing whistles of the trains,
and the birches that were as though
they had been released from the camps,
and were hobbling out onto the field,

and the secret midnight gathering
of the huge Biblical oaks,
and the half-sunk boat that
sailed out from someone's dreams...
Early winter already wandered around
slightly whitening these ploughed fields
and unintentionally reduced all the distances
to an impenetrable murk.
It seemed that after the end
there would never be anything.
Who is wandering again near the porch
calling us by name?
Who has pressed his face against the icy glass of the window
and is waving his hand like a wind-blown branch?...
In response in the cobwebbed corner
a sunbeam dances in the mirror.

[Leningrad, 1960]

Speed

This disaster knows no limit.
You, who have no soul and no body,
alighted on the world like an evil vulture
and disfigured everything and governed everything,
        and took – nothing.

[1959]

'These praises do not become me'

These praises do not become me,
and talk about Sappho is quite out of place.
I know there is another motive for this,
but you and I will not read about it.

Let some save their skins by running away,
and others nod from pedestals,
but these poems had an undercurrent
so powerful that it was like looking
into an abyss that drew one down and in,
and you could never reach the bottom,
and its empty silence would
never grow tired of talking.

[1959]

Echo

The roads to the past have long been closed,
and what is the past to me now?
What is there? Bloody slabs,
or a bricked up door,
or an echo that still could not
keep quiet, although I ask so...
The same thing happened with that echo
as with the one I carry in my heart.

[1960]

Masquerade Chatter

In an ordinary envelope
a tiny, filled-out sheet of paper
enumerated the mass dead,
not coded as a cryptogram,
yet an invisible torrent of non-being
is dispassionately founded on it.

[March 1961]

216

Three Verses

I. *'It's time to forget the camels' din'*

It's time to forget the camels' din,
and the white house in Tashkent on Zhukovsky Street.
It's time, time to go to the birches and the mushrooms,
to the expansive, Moscow autumn.
There all is shining, all is in dew,
and the sky clambers high,
and the Rogachev highway remembers
the robber whistling of the young Blok...

[1944–1950]

II. *'Rummaging in your black memory you find'*

Rummaging in your black memory you find
long evening-gloves,
and the Petersburg night. And in the dark of the theatre boxes
that stifling, sweet smell.
Wind from the gulf. And there between the lines,
shunning the 'ahs' and 'ohs',
Blok will smile at you contemptuously –
the tragic tenor of the age.

[1960(?)]

III. *'Blok is right'*

Blok is right – again the lamp, the chemist's,
the Neva, silence, granite...
That man stands there –
like a memorial to the beginning of the century
Saying farewell to Pushkin House
he gave up everything as lost
and accepted death's tranquillity
as an undeserved rest.

[7 June 1946]

'I was wrongly captivated'

I was wrongly captivated
by the splendid dance of disaster:
everything was like that then,
then everything was like that.
. . . .
I slept in the queen's bed,
starved, carried firewood,
but my head was never turned
by praise or damnation.

[13 August 1960]

'We did not face the disasters together in vain'

We did not face the disasters together in vain,
without any hope of a breathing space –
they were sworn in and voted
and calmly continued on their way.

But perhaps in vain did I remain pure
as a candle before the Lord –
together with you I writhed at the feet
of the bloody puppet-executioner.

No! not under a foreign sky,
not under the shelter of alien wings –
I was with my people then,
there where my people were doomed to be.

[1961]

218

From Black Songs

Words to shame you
                    I. Annensky

I.

It's right that he did not take me with him
or call me his girl friend.
For him I became a song, a fate,
transparent sleeplessness and snowstorm.
You would not recognise me
at the city railway station
as that, alas, young-looking,
practical, Parisian woman.

II.

In spite of all your promises
you took the ring from my finger
and forgot me in the very depths.
You couldn't help me in any way.
Then why tonight did you send me
your spirit again?
He was handsome, young and red-haired.
He was like a woman,
whispered about Rome, beckoned me to Paris,
howled like a hired mourner.
He couldn't live without me any longer:
come shame, or prison...

I managed without him.

[1960]

'Under the most sacred maple'

Under the most sacred maple, I grant you
a far from simple conversation,
silence with a silver ring,
the clear well water –
and there's no need to answer
with a suffering groan...I agree, but wait,
there was a mysterious heat of foreboding
in this dark green darkness.

[Komarovo, 1961]

Listening to Singing

The woman's voice rushes like the wind,
black, moist, and nocturnal.
Whatever it touches in flight
becomes something else immediately.
It flows like the sparkle of diamonds,
silvers something somewhere –
mysterious rustles
of rarest silk.
Such a powerful force
is embodied in the enchanted voice,
as though a secret flight of stairs
lies ahead and not the grave.

[Lenin Hospital, 19 December 1961]

(Vishnevskaya was singing Villa Lobos' 'Brazil Bachiana')

A Page of Ancient History

The Death of Sophokles

Then the king learnt that Sophokles was dead
(Legend)

That night an eagle flew from the heavens to Sophokles' house,
and the mournful choir of cicadas suddenly rang out in the
garden.
At that hour the genius was already passing into immortality,
skirting the enemy camp by the walls of his native town.
And this was when the king had a strange dream:
Dionysus himself ordered him to raise the siege,
so as not to let the noise disturb the burial rites,
and allow the Athenians the joy of honouring him.

[1961]

Alexander at Thebes

The young king must have been terrible and menacing
as he pronounced: 'You will destroy Thebes.'
And the old leader beheld that proud city,
as he had known it once of old.
Put it all, all to the fire. And the king counted
the towers, the gates, the temples – a wonder of the world,
but suddenly he paused, his face lit up and he said:
'Only make sure that the house of the Poet is not touched.'

[1961]

'Those "unforgettable dates" have come round'

Those 'unforgettable dates' have come round again,
and every single one of them is cursed.

But most accursed of them is this rising dawn...
and I know that the heart does not beat faster in vain.

It is flooded with a murky anguish
in the ringing moment before the storm at sea.

I've given up the past for lost,
what do you want my comrade south-west wind?

that the lime trees and maples should burst into my room,
green, like a gipsy camp, bustling riotously,

and the water roll up to the bridges' belly –
everything like then, like then eternally.

[Fountain House, Leningrad, 1944]

Petersburg in 1913

The barrel-organ wails in the suburbs.
They are dragging the bear along, and the gipsy woman
dances on the spit-strewn pavement.
The steam-train goes as far
as the Church of the Virgin in Mourning,
and its ache-making whistle
echoes over the Neva.
There's anger and unbridled will in the black wind.
From here it's only a short way to the Hot Field.
Here my prophetic voice will fall silent.
Furthermore, here miracles are more savage.
But let's go away – I cannot wait around.

[1961]

'If everyone in the world'

If everyone in the world
who asked for spiritual help from me,
all the holy fools, the dumb,
the abandoned wives and cripples,
the convicts and suicides –
each sent me one kopeck,
I would be 'richer than all in Egypt',
as the late Kuzmin used to say.
But they didn't send me one kopeck,
instead they shared their strength with me.
And I became the strongest person in the world,
so that even *this* is not difficult for me.

Tsarskoye Selo Ode
The 1900s

> *A plank fence in a side-street...*
> N. Gumilyov

The real ode
came in a whisper...Hold on,
I'll hide the narcotic of Tsarskoye Selo
in the empty drawer,
in the fateful casket,
in the 'Cypress Chest'.
That side-street
is coming to an end.
Here it isn't Temnik or Shuya,
but the town of parks and hills,
and I will describe it to you
as Chagall painted his Vitebsk.
Here they used to walk with a military swagger,
the chestnut horse trotted along,
and here was an excellent inn
even before the first railway came.

The street lamps flooded
the objects with a matt light,
and the silhouette
of the court carriage flashed past.
How I wish that the off-blue snowdrifts
might appear with Petersburg in the distance.
Here there are no ancient treasures,
just a plank fence,
the quartermaster's stores
and the coachmen's yard.
There a young she-devil
lisps awkwardly, and barely
manages to tell fortunes for the guests.
There the soldiers' jokes flow
with undiminished venom...
The striped sentry box,
and a stream of coarse tobacco smoke.
They bawled out songs
and swore by the priest's wife,
drank the tsar's vodka till late
then ate funeral cake.
The rook cawed and praised
this ghostly world...
The huge cuirassier
drove on his sledge.

[Komarovo, 3 August 1961]

224

Our Own Land

There is no one in the world more tearless,
more proud, more simple than us.
1922

We don't wear it in sacred amulets on our chests.
We don't compose hysterical poems about it.
It does not disturb our bitter dream-sleep.
It doesn't seem to be the promised paradise.
We don't make of it a soul
object for sale and barter,
and we being sick, poverty-stricken, unable to utter a word
don't even remember about it.
Yes, for us it's mud on galoshes,
    for us it's crunch on teeth,
    and we mill, mess and crush
    that dust and ashes
    that is not mixed up in anything.
But we'll lie in it and be it,
that's why, so freely, we call it our own.

[Leningrad, 1961]

The Last Rose

You will write about us in your slanting handwriting
J. Brodsky

I should bow to pray with Morozova,
dance with Herod's stepdaughter,
fly in smoke from Dido's funeral pyre,
to be with Joan on her pyre.
Oh Lord! Don't you see I'm tired
of resurrecting, dying and living.
Take everything – just let me feel again
the freshness of this crimson rose.

[Komarovo, 9 August 1962]

A Wreath for the Dead

I. *The Master*
To the Memory of Innokenty Annensky

He whom I consider the master,
passed like a shadow and left no shadow.
He swallowed all the poison, drank the narcotic,
and waited for fame, but could not wait long enough.
He, who was the portent, the omen,
had compassion for everyone, instilled tranquillity in everyone
then he choked.

[1945]

II.

De profundis...My generation
did not taste much honey. And now
only the wind wails in the distance,
only memory sings of the dead.
Our business was unfinished,
our hours were numbered,
up to the longed-for watershed,
up to the summit of the great spring,
up to the frenzied blossoming –
all that was left was a brief breathing space...
Two wars, my generation,
lit your terrible path.

[Tashkent, 1944]

III. *In Memory of M.A. Bulgakov*

Look, this is for you, instead of roses to your grave,
instead of incense smoke.
You lived so sternly and to the end
were unswerving in your grand contempt.

226

You drank wine, your wit was incomparable;
you felt claustrophobic indoors,
and you invited in a terrible guest,
and stayed with her alone.
Now you do not exist, and everything around is silent
about your mournful, lofty life,
only my voice, like a flute, will be heard
at your speech-less funeral feast.
O, who would dare to believe that it would fall upon me,
half out of my mind, upon me, the mourner of the days of
        the dead,
upon me, smouldering on a slow fire,
who had lost everyone, who had forgotten everything, –
to write *in memoriam* of him who full of strength,
and bright ideas, and will,
seemed to be talking to me only yesterday,
in pain, knowing he was going to die, and hiding it.

IV. *In Memory of Boris Pilnyak*

You alone will guess the meaning of all this...
When the sleepless darkness seethes all around,
that sunny wedge of lilies of the valley
bursts into the December night.
I am walking to you on the forest path.
You are laughing carefree.
But the fir wood and the reeds of the pond
echo back to me strangely...
Oh, if by this I should wake the dead,
forgive me – I can do no other;
I mourn you as my own
and envy anyone who cries,
who can cry in this terrible hour
for those who lie there at the bottom of the ravine...
Tears could not reach my eyes,
could not refresh them – they simply boiled dry.

[1938]

H

V. *To Osip Mandelstam*

I bend to your poems as to the chalice –
they are incalculably dear to me. –
They bring the black, tender news
of our bloodied youth.

Once at night I breathed in
the same air as you, over the same abyss.
In that empty, iron night:
you can scream and call out, but it is all in vain.

How spicy the carnations smelled
that I once dreamed of there;
there where Eurydices circled round,
and the bull carries Europa over the waves;

there where our shadows rush
over the Neva, the Neva, the Neva,
there where the Neva splashes on the steps –
it is your passport to immortality.

It is the dear keys of a flat,
of which there's not a blind trace left...
It is the voice of a mysterious lyre
that is visiting a meadow beyond the grave.

[1957]

VI. *Late Answer*
To Marina Tsvetayeva

> *My white handed one, my black witch...*

Invisible one, double, mocking-bird,
why do you hide in the black bushes,
then shelter in a ramshackle starling-box,
then flit over the crosses of the dead,
then cry from the Marinka tower:

'I returned home today,
look on in wonder, my native fields,
at what happened to me after this.
The deep has swallowed up my loved ones,
the father's house is pillaged.'
You and I today, Marina,
are walking through the midnight capital,
and millions like us are following behind us.
There is no more silent procession,
and round about the funeral bells ring,
and wild Moscow wails
as the blizzard covers our tracks.

[Fountain House, 16 March 1940]

VII.   *To Boris Pasternak*

1.

The autumn advances like Tamerlane,
silence in the Arbat backstreets.
The no-through-road looms beyond
the railway station or the mist.

So here it is, the last one. The frenzy
abates. It is as if the world's gone deaf.
The powerful old age has the quality of the Gospel,
and that most bitter Gethsemane sigh.

[Fountain House, 1947]

2.

Yesterday an unrepeatable voice fell silent,
and he who talked and listened to the forests went away.
He turned into the life-giving ear of corn,
or the fine rain that he sang of.
And all the flowers that ever flowered in the world
burst into bloom to meet his death.

But suddenly a silence fell
on the planet with the humble name...Earth.

[1960]

3.

As Antigone led the blind Oedipus,
so the Muse led the seer to death.
Just one crazed lime tree
blossomed in the mourning May
right opposite the window, by which
he once confided in me that a golden,
winged road twisted before him,
where he was protected by the supreme will.

[Botkin Hospital, Moscow, 11 June 1960]

VIII. *There are Four of Us*
Komarovo Drafts

> *Are all the torments in Dante*
> *destined for the supple gipsy*
> *woman?*
>> Osip Mandelstam

> *This is how I see your image*
> *and look.*
>> Boris Pasternak

> *O, Muse of Lamentation...*
>> Marina Tsvetayeva

And here I retired from everything,
from every earthly blessing.
The gnarled forest root
became the guardian spirit of this place.

In life we are all in a way guests,
living is only a habit.
I seem to hear across the reaches of space
two voices calling each other.

230

Two? And still by an Eastern wall,
above the raspberry canes,
the dark, fresh branch of elderberry...
That is a letter from Marina.

[In Gavan' Leningrad (in delirium), November 1961]

IX. *In Memory of M.M. Zoshchenko*

It's as if I hear his distant voice,
but there is nothing, and no one around.
You will put his body
into the black, good earth.
Neither granite, nor the weeping willow
will shade his featherlight ashes –
only the sea winds from the gulf
will fly in to mourn him.

[Komarovo, 1958]

X. *In Memory of Anta*

Though this may be from another cycle...
I see clear eyes smiling
and 'she's dead' settled so mournfully
on her dear nickname, as though I heard it
for the first time.

XI. *In Memory of N. Punin*

His heart no longer attends
my voice, in triumph or in shame.
It's all over...My song rushes
into the empty night – where you have ceased to be.

[1953]

XII. *Tsarskoye Selo Lines*

The autumn wind blows in
the fifth act of the play.
In the park every flower-bed
seems to be a fresh grave.
The funeral feast has been celebrated,
and there's nothing left to do.
Why do I slow down as if waiting for
the miracle to come about?
It takes little effort to hold back
the boat before it leaves the quay,
as you say goodbye to someone
who's staying behind.

[1944]

Twenty-three Years Later

I put out those sacred candles,
my magical evening is over –
the executioners, the pretenders, the predecessors
and, alas, the public prosecutors' speeches –
everything passes; and I dream of you
dancing your heart out before the Ark,
beyond the rain, wind and snow.
Your shadow is over the immortal shore.
Your voice comes from the depth of the darkness,
and insistently you call my name:
'Anna!'
just as intimately as before.

In Memory of V.S. Sreznevskaya

It almost cannot be, you were always there for me:
in the shade of the blessed lime trees, in the blockade and the
      hospital,
in the prison cell and where the evil birds were
and the wild grasses and the terrifying water.
Oh how everything changed, but you were always there,
and I feel that half my soul has been amputated,
the half that was you – in it I found an important
cause. Then suddenly everything was forgotten...
But your ringing voice calls me from there
and asks me not to be sad and to wait for death like a miracle.
Well – I'll try!

[Komarovo, 9 September 1964]

The North

The West spread slander, and believed in it.
The East betrayed luxuriously,
the South gave me short rations of air,
grinning between the bold lines.
But the clover was almost knee-deep;
the moist moon played on a pearl horn:
thus my faithful old friend the North
consoled me as only it could.
I pined away in exhaustion,
I suffocated in the stench and blood,
I could no longer live in this house...
That was when iron Finland spoke to me:
'You'll find everything except happiness.
But it doesn't matter, just keep living!'

[1964]

Christmas Eve
Last Day in Rome

The conclusion of a cycle that never was
is often hardest on the heart.
I have grown out of much in life,
I need hardly anything –

for me the Komarovo pines
speak in their own tongues
and springs linger and stand out from one another,
reflected in puddles that have drunk of the sky.

[1964]

From an Italian Diary

It was a mistake for us to see that year in,
absolutely wrong.
My God, what did you and I do?
With whom did we exchange fates?

It would be better for us not to be alive,
better to be in heaven's Kremlin citadel –
we flew like birds and bloomed like flowers,
but we were still, just you and I.

[1964]

Imitation of the Korean

I scored a rare success: I dreamed
of someone almost like you.
And I woke up in tears,

234

calling you out of the darkness.
But the one I saw was taller and stronger,
perhaps even younger,
and did not know the secrets
of our terrible days. My God, help me!
What? It was a ghost,
as I foretold half a century ago.
But I was waiting for a man
till all my powers were lost.

In Vyborg

Huge steps underwater
lead to Neptune's kingdom.
Here Scandinavia is frozen
like a shadow, all in one blinding apparition.
Wordless the song, dumb the music,
but the air is burning with their scent
and the white winter on its knees
watches over everything in its prayer vigil.

[24 September 1964]

Fragment

This is where you ought to roam,
shadow of a shadow, someone else's fiancée.
Could you not find a happier
place in which to promenade?
Early winter already wandered around
slightly whitening these ploughed fields
and unintentionally reduced all the distances
to an impenetrable murk.
Was it so bad by the dark, green sea,
that you were forced to bow to a terrible fate
and embark on this without putting up a fight?

You are the most forbidden rose,
you are twice-crowned to rule.
The first frost will kill you here.
. . . .
The dome is on its side,
puddles, sounds of geese and trains.
The little poplar, burnt by the moon,
stretches crucified arms to the sky.
The enigmatic emeralds of stars,
the rustle underfoot of piles
of rusty, rotting, fragrant leaves.
But the enchanted shadow is silent
and answers me not a word.

'The ice grows thick on the windowpanes'

The ice grows thick on the windowpanes.
The clock insists: 'Don't be cowardly!'
Even dead, I fear
to hear what is coming to me.

I beg the door as though it were an idol:
'Do not let disaster in!'
Who is howling like a beast hiding in
the garden beyond the wall?

[1965]

'No, we are not playing'

No, we are not playing
chess or tennis.
This game has another name,
if it needs a name.

Not parting or meeting,
not conversation, not silence...
And that's why your blood
turns a little cold.

'A strange companion'

A strange companion was sent to me from hell,
a guest from an unbelievable abyss.
It seemed the birds fell silent, the flowers died
under his eyes' stare. Death
blossomed in him with a sort of black life.
His madness and wisdom were destructive.

Couplets

Who sent him here,
bursting out from all mirrors?

*

I found no answer in the depths of the music,
silence fell again, and the ghost of summer appeared.

*

I buried all the unburied ones.
I mourned everyone, but who will mourn me?

*

Don't give me anything to remember you by,
I know how short memory is.

*

Pray to the night that you
won't wake up famous in the morning.

On the Road

A land not our own
and yet eternally memorable,
and in the sea there is tender-iced
and fresh water.

On the bottom – sand whiter than chalk,
and the air is drunk as wine,
and the rose-pink mass of the pines
is laid bare in the sunset hour.

The sunset itself in the sea air
is such that I cannot tell
if this is the end of the day or of the world,
or the secret of secrets is within me again.

[1964]

A HALF CENTURY
OF QUATRAINS

'A Half Century of Quatrains'

White, empty days round Christmas.
Whirl snowstorm, whirl.
I don't care if the streets are icy –
I've got no one to go to.

[January 1914]

Someone's pine coffin is carried –
somebody will be happy with God,
but I am concerned with small things
and my shelter on earth is cramped.

*

Hurtful talk does not bother me.
I don't blame anyone for anything.
Give me a non-shameful end
to my shameful life.

*

The tomtits sing well,
the peacock has a bright tail.
But there's no sweeter bird
than the fabled 'Alkonost'.

*

How strange that we knew him?
He was miserly in his praise, but a stranger to abuse and anger.
The Sacred Maiden looked after
her beautiful poet.

[August 1921]

*

It irks me to keep
people away from me.
It irks me to call down blessings
on friends I don't even know.

*

Here the most beautiful girls argue
for the honour of getting married to an executioner.
Here they torture the just ones at night
and starve to death those who won't break.

[1924]

*

I will wander here at night,
an unmourned shadow,
where the star rays play
like lilac blossoms.

[Sheremetev Garden, 1920s]

*

I am in no wise a prophet.
My life flows clear as a river.
I just do not want to sing
to the clank of prison keys.

[1930s]

*

All that's left of your earthly possessions
is your daily bread alone,
kind, human words
and the clear voice of the field.

*

Living – in freedom,
dying – at home.
Wolf Field,
yellow straw.

[22 June 1941: Declaration of War]

*

Dig my shovel,
ring out my pickaxe,
we will not let the Satan
into our peaceful fields.

*

Go off again into the thickets of the night
where the vagabond nightingale sings
sweeter than honey, sweeter than strawberries,
sweeter even than my jealousy.

*

I'll not take my eyes off the horizon
where the snowstorms dance wildly.
My friend, three fronts separate us:
ours, the enemy's and ours again.

[Tashkent,1942–1943]

*

When, by habit, I call over
the names of my dearest friends,
it is always the silence
that answers my strange roll-call.

[Tashkent, 8 November 1943]

*

Another Afterword to the *Leningrad Cycle*

Was it not I at the foot of the cross,
was it not I who drowned in the sea,
oh grief, did my lips
forget your taste.

[16 January 1944]

One more Afterword to the *Leningrad Cycle*

...I hand over my silence –
my last and highest award –
to the great martyr
                    Leningrad.

[Tashkent, 16 January 1944]

*

From the strange poetry, whose each step is a secret,
where precipices are left and right,
where fame is underfoot like a withered leaf,
there would seem to be no salvation.

[Autumn 1944]

*

Russian seems not enough for you,
and you want to know in all languages
how steep the rises and falls are
and what is the price of conscience – and terror.

*

I'll grant forgiveness to all,
and at the Resurrection of Christ
I will kiss those who betrayed me on the forehead,
and those who didn't – on the lips.

*

Go on, call me today,
I know you're out there somewhere,
I feel totally abandoned
and hear no winged message.

*

He went away from me as though I were 'that countess'
down the winding staircase
to see the terrible, blue, dawn hour
over the terrible Neva.

[1958]

*

Sick – laid up in bed for three months,
death I didn't seem to fear.
In delirium I seem to myself to be
a chance stranger in this terrible body.

*

You will not be responsible for my fate.
You can sleep sound for the time being.
Might is right, but your children
will curse you for me.

*

Perhaps later you did hate
and regretted not having killed.
You alone did not hurt me,
and by not having hurt – destroyed.

*

We taught ourselves not to meet any more,
now even our eyes don't meet,
but we ourselves could not vouch for
what would happen to us within the hour.

[1964]

*

I am going where I need nothing,
where my dearest companion is just a shadow,
and the wind wafts from the muffled garden,
but the grave is a step away.

[1964]

*

From a Diary of a Journey
Occasional Poem

Dawn breaks – it's the Last Judgement.
Meeting is more bitter than parting.
There your living hands
hand me over to posthumous fame.

[December 1964]

*

Your crazed eyes
and icy words,
and declarations of love
even before the first meeting.

*

What, only ten years, my God you must be joking!
You came back so quickly.
I just didn't expect it from the way we parted,
some strange foreign winter.

*

The mad face of the black music
will appear for a moment and vanish in the dark.
But I divined mysterious signs –
I am wearing my black ring again.

*

They had already drunk the fierce wine
of fornication to the dregs.
Not for them to see the pure face of truth
or know tears of repentance.

*

Who sent him here so unexpectedly
out from all those mirrors?
Innocent night, silent night...
Death has sent the bridegroom.

*

I'll exchange the shining and the glory
of the stars' flock
for the lily-of-the-valley May
in my Moscow of the dreaming domes.

*

Suffering is my Muse,
who somehow passed through with me
to an impossible land, where parting lives,
and where there's a she-vulture who's known the taste of evil.

*

When the music burst forth
and winter woke with a start,
I realised that Queen Death
was at the mooring.

[1965–1966]

*

246

EPIC AND
DRAMATIC
FRAGMENTS

Epic Motifs

1.

At that time I was a guest on earth.
I was christened: Anna,
sweetest sound for people's lips and ears.
I felt such joy in living
that I didn't count just twelve holidays
but as many as there were days in the year.
I obeyed secret orders
and chose a free comrade
and loved only the sun and the trees.
Once in late summer I met
a foreign woman at the crafty sunset hour.
Together we bathed in the warm sea.
Her clothes seemed strange to me,
stranger still her lips, and her words
were like shooting stars in the September night.
The tall one taught me to swim
holding up my inexperienced body
with one arm on the dense waves.
As we stood in the blue water
she used to talk unhurriedly with me
and it seemed to me, treetops
rustled slightly, sand rasped
or bagpipes in a silver voice
sang distantly of the evening of parting.
But I couldn't remember her words,
and often woke up at night in pain,
and seemed to see her parted lips,
her eyes and smooth hair.
I prayed to the sad girl
as though she were a messenger from heaven:
'Tell me, tell me why my memory has died?
Your words have touched me so fondly and painfully,
but you've taken away from me the bliss of remembering them.'
Only once while I was picking
grapes and filling a wicker basket
and the beauty sat on the grass,

her eyes closed, her hair flowing loose,
languid and languishing
from the scent of the heavy black grapes,
and the fresh tang of the wild mint,
she implanted wonderful words
into the treasury of my memory,
and I dropped the full basket
and fell to the dry, fragrant ground
as though to a lover when love sings.

2.

I left the woods of my sacred homeland
and the house, where the Muse of Lamentation pined away,
and happy and calm I lived
on a low island, which was like a raft,
moored in the rich Neva delta.
Oh, the mysterious days of winter,
dear work, light tiredness,
and roses in the jug!
The short side-street was covered in snow.
The church of St Catharine's
altar wall was right next door.
I would leave the house so early,
often over untrodden snow,
searching in vain for my tracks of yesterday,
over the pale, clean swaddling snow,
and by the side of the river where the schooners
snuggled up to each other tenderly like doves
longing for spring by the grey shore
I would walk to the old bridge.
There was a room, like a cage,
up near the roof of the dirty, noisy house,
where he would whistle like a siskin as he painted,
and complain happily and speak so sadly
about the happiness that never came.
I used to look fearfully at the grey canvas
as though into a mirror, and as each week passed
my likeness to the painting
became more bitter, more strange.
Now I do not know where my artist friend is,

249

with whom I climbed from the blue attic
out of the window onto the roof,
and walked along the ledge above the death-drop,
to see the snow, the Neva and the clouds;
but I feel that our Muses are friends
in a carefree, enticing friendship,
like girls who have not known love.

3.

Twilight falls and in the dark blue sky,
where such a short time ago the Temple in Jerusalem
shone in mysterious grandeur,
just two stars over the confusion of branches,
and somehow the snow falls, not from above,
but as though it is rising from the earth,
lazy, caressing, and cautious.
That day my usual walk was a strange one.
When I went out a transparent reflection
on things and faces blinded me,
as though everywhere lay petals
of those delicate, yellow-pink roses
whose name I forget.
The windless, dry, frosty air
so cherished and preserved each word
that it seemed to me silence did not exist.
The children on the bridge, thrusting
their mittened hands through the rusty railings,
fed the hungry, colourful ducks
that ducked and dived in the ink-black hole in the ice.
I thought, it's impossible
that I shall ever forget this.
And if a difficult road lay before me
here is a light burden I am forced
to carry, so that in old age, in sickness,
perhaps even in poverty I'd remember
the furious sunset, fullness
of spiritual powers and the dear charm of life.

[1914–1916]

NORTHERN ELEGIES

All in sacrifice to the memory of you
Pushkin

The First
Prehistory

> *I don't live there now...*
> Pushkin

Dostoyevsky's Russia. The moon
is almost a quarter hid by the bell-tower.
The inns are open. The cabs fly.
The five storey blocks grow
in Gorokhovaya, in Znamenya, round Smolny.
Dancing classes everywhere, moneychangers' shop signs,
and alongside: 'Henriette', 'Basile', 'André',
and the ornate coffins of 'Shumilov the Elder'.
And yet the city has changed little.
Others as well as myself,
have noticed it can sometimes
resemble an old lithograph,
not first class, but perfectly decent,
of, it seems, the seventies.
Especially in winter, before dawn,
or at dusk, beyond the gates,
the hard, straight Liteyny is dark,
not yet disfigured by modernisation,
and opposite me live Nekrasov
and Saltykov – both on memorial plaques.
Oh how terrible it would be for them
to see those plaques. I pass on.
The ditches in the Karamazovs' village are lush,
and the summerhouses are derelict in the little gardens,
and the glass in the windows is black as an ice-hole.
It seems something happened there
that it's better not to guess at, let's pass on.
One cannot always arrange things so that every place
should open its secret to us,
(and I cannot visit Father Seraphim at Optina Shrine...)

Rustle of skirts, check plaids,
hazel wood frames of the mirrors
that are struck by Anna Karenina's beauty,
and in the narrow corridors that wallpaper
which we so loved in childhood;
the same plush chairs
by the light of the yellow kerosene lamp...
Everything intellectual but not bourgeois, slapdash, anyhow...
Fathers and grandfathers are misunderstood.
Lands are mortgaged. There's roulette in Baden-Baden.
And a woman with transparent eyes,
(of such a deep blue that when you looked into them
it was impossible not to think of the sea).
with the unusual name 'Inna' and a white little hand,
and a kindness which
I seem to have inherited from her:
a useless gift in my cruel life...

The country is running a fever, and Dostoyevsky, the Omsk
                convict
understood everything and gave everything up for lost.
Now he will transform everything
and will himself soar over the primordial chaos
like some spirit. Midnight strikes.
The pen squeaks, and many pages are tainted
with the stench of the Semyonov parade-ground.
So that was when we took it into our heads to be born,
and unerringly having measured time
so as to miss nothing of those unprecedented spectacles,
we said farewell to our non-being.

[Leningrad, 3 September 1940
Tashkent, October 1943]

The Second
(About the 1910s)

I had no rosy childhood
with curls, freckles and teddy bears,
no nice aunties and fearsome uncles,

no friends even among the river pebbles.
Right from the very beginning
it seemed to me that I myself was
in a sort of dream or delirium,
or a reflection in someone else's mirror,
nameless, fleshless, motiveless.
I already knew the list of crimes
which I had to carry out.
So pacing around like a sleepwalker
I walked into life and it terrified me:
and it spread out before me like the meadow
where Proserpina once strolled.
Unexpected doors opened
to me, who was homeless and awkward,
and the people came out and shouted:
'She's come. It's her!'
And I looked at them in crazed disbelief
and thought: 'They're out of their minds!'
And the more loudly they praised me,
the more pressingly the people enthused about me,
the more terrible it was to live in the world,
and the more intense was the longing to wake up,
and I knew that I would pay a hundredfold,
in prison, in the grave, in the madhouse,
everywhere where it is fated for people
like me to wake up – but the torture by happiness continued.

[Moscow, 4 July 1955]

The Third

It was terrifying living in that home.
Neither the patriarchal hearth,
nor the tiny cradle of my child,
nor the fact that we were both young
and full of ideas and that success
did not dare go a step away
from our door for seven long years,
could diminish the feeling of terror.

I learned to laugh at it
and left a drop of wine
and a crust of bread for him who scratched
like a dog at the door at night,
or looked in at the low window
there where we, suddenly fell silent, and tried
not to see what was happening the other side of the mirror,
and under whose heavy boots
the steps of the dark staircase groaned
as though pitifully praying for mercy.
And you said, with a strange smile:
'Who are *they* carrying down the stairs?'

Now you are there where everything is known, tell me:
what lived in this home apart from us?

[Tsarskoye Selo, 1921]

The Fourth

So here it is that autumn landscape
that I have feared so much all my life;
the sky like a flaming chasm,
the sounds of the city – like sounds
heard from the afterlife and forever alien.
As though all that I fought inside me
throughout my life has taken on
a separate existence and is incarnate
in these blind walls and this black garden...
And at that moment, behind my back,
my old house was still following me
with a screwed up malevolent eye:
its window that I can never forget.
Fifteen years – as though they pretended
to be fifteen granite centuries.
But I myself was like granite;
now pray, torment youself, call me
sea princess. It doesn't matter, forget it...
But I had to assure myself

that this had all happened many times,
and not to me alone, but to others also —
and, for them, even worse. No, not worse — better.
And my voice — this perhaps was
the most fearful thing — spoke out of the darkness:
'Fifteen years ago, with what song did you
meet this day? You begged the heavens,
the chorus of stars, the chorus of waters
to greet your solemn meeting
with him whom you left today...
So, here is your silver wedding:
call the guests, let your beauty shine, celebrate!'

[Tashkent, March 1942]

The Fifth

The harsh epoch
turned me back like a river.
My life has been deliberately changed
and flows along another channel;
past that other course,
and I do not know my banks.
Oh, how many spectacles have I missed,
the curtain has risen without me,
and likewise fallen. How many friends
of mine have I never met once in my life,
and how many plans of towns
could draw tears from my eyes.
I know only one city in the world
and can find my way round it by feel in my sleep.
How many poems have I not written,
and their secret chorus wanders around me
and perhaps will still
suffocate me...
I know the beginnings and the endings
and life after the end, and something
which there is no need to recollect.
Some other woman took over

my unique place,
carries my most lawful name,
leaving me a nickname out of which
I have made, I suppose, all I could.
Oh God, even my grave will not be my own.

But sometimes the mad, spring wind,
or a combination of words in a book picked up by chance,
or some smile or other will suddenly draw
me in to my non-existent life.

Such and such might have happened in that year,
something else in this year: travelling, seeing, thinking,
and remembering, entering into a new love,
as if in the mirror were reflected the dulled
consciousness of betrayal and a wrinkle that was not there
yesterday.

. . . .

But if from somewhere outside
I looked in on my present life,
I would at last realise what envy means.

[Leningrad, 2 September 1945]

The Sixth

Memories have three epochs.
And the first is like yesterday.
The soul is under their blessed, protective skies
and the body basks in their shadow.
Laughter has not died down and the tears stream,
the ink stain is unwiped on the table,
the kiss is imprinted on the heart,
unique, parting, unforgettable...
But this does not last for long...
The protective skies are no longer overhead, and somewhere
in the dull suburbs there is a lonely house,

256

where it's cold in winter and hot in summer,
where a spider lives and the dust is everywhere,
where passionate letters burn to ash,
portraits change stealthily,
and people visit it as though a grave,
and wash their hands when they get home,
and shake off a fleeting tear
from tired eyelids, and sigh heavily...
But the clocks tick, one spring
replaces another, the sky turns rose-pink,
names of cities change,
and eye-witnesses of events are no longer,
and there is no one to cry with, no one to reminisce with.
And shadows pass slowly from us
which we no longer call upon,
whose return would be terrible to us.
Once awake, we see that we have forgotten
the very road that led to the lonely house,
and choking with anger and shame,
we run to it, but (as in a dream)
everything is different there:
people, things, walls;
and nobody knows us; we are strangers.
We went to the wrong place...Oh God!
Now comes the most bitter moment:
we realise that we could not contain
this past in the frontiers of our life,
and it is almost as alien to us
as to our neighbour in the flat;
we could not recognise those who have died,
and those whom God parted from us
got on fine without us – perhaps
everything's been for the best.

[Leningrad, 5 February 1945]

From Prologue: A Play
Fragments from a Tragedy or a Dream within a Dream

She Speaks

No, there can be no one in the world
more shelterless, more homeless.
I come to you as the voice of the lute
through the ghostly dawn beyond the grave.
You will learn to fight with yourself,
you who leaned into my last dream.
Curse again the creak of the bucket on the well,
the rustle of the pines,
the black cawing of crows,
the earth on which I trod,
the yellow star in my window,
what I was and what I became,
and the time when I said to you
that I had seemed to see you in my dream.
Other words appear to me
in the curses that you breathe:
they are tighter, more intoxicating than embraces
and tender as the first grass shoots.

He Speaks

Dear sister of the riverside willows,
though you are more charming than the angels,
I will murder you with my song,
not spilling a drop of blood on this earth.
I will not touch you.
Without a look I will fall out of love with you
and I will quench my thirst at last
on your incredible gasp.
You will deliver me from her,
who wandered over the earth before me,
sterner than ice, more fiery than fire,
who dwells now in the ether.

He Speaks

Whoever's wife you were to become
our marriage in crime
would continue
because I shared with you
the darkness of Creation.
I don't conceal it now.
But then we hid it from each other,
from others, from God, from the end.
I remember our place in Dante's circle
as though it were the victor's crown of laurel.
I saw you – the bride in the church,
I saw you – alive on the burning pyre,
I saw you – stoned to death,
and a plaything in the devil's game.
You looked me in the eyes from everywhere.
You called me from everywhere, and you gave me your soul;
and your body you gave back to God in sacrifice.
You alone were my fate.
I was ready to do everything for you.
My God, what we did together in that utterly
final dream layer.
Was I your murderer or were you mine?
I can't remember anything...
As a Roman, Scythian, Byzantine,
I was a witness to your shame.
You know that I'd agree to do anything:
to curse, to forget, to hand over to the enemy.
Let there be light in the darkness, let sin be beautiful –
there's just one thing I cannot do –
that I cannot even say
or endure in mourning –
I would rather search for your grave
than face the fact that you never existed.
But there is a simple, towering truth:
I died, and you were never born...
Our union may have been sinful, criminal,
holy – but it had to be.

259

J

She Speaks

However many tortures another man invented for me,
I was never faithful to him.
But I drink your jealousy, constantly
like a magic potion.

*

This paradise where we have not sinned
makes us feel sick:
the scent of the death-bringing lilies
and shame that has not realised the quality of shame.
Eve smiles as she dreams
that a lover's hand will lead her
through the terrible ages
with the future murderer in her womb.

Let me go for just one moment,
so that I can laugh, or simply be,
lest I imagine an octopus has caught me
in the midnight sea's depths.
I know that your throat was parched,
that you were burnt out and couldn't breathe,
and that the wings of night
beat at your door.

*   *   *   *

The world has never known such poverty.
It knows no creature with fewer rights.
Even the wind outside the broken shutter
speaks to me overfamiliarly.

First Voice

We tasted the forbidden fruit of knowledge,
and in the bottomless abysses of consciousness
buildings became all the more transparent and terrifying
and the last hour shows through them.

Second Voice

And now the distant thunder rumbles...
Will what we call *music*,
for lack of a better name,
        save us?

Heard in the Distance

Your caresses cause terror, your entreaties are insults,
        you don't knock when you come in.
It will be wonderful all the way with you,
        even parting.
Let the crimson foam spread
        over evil fate,
but even betrayal will sound to you
        like a solemn oath.
She has found out the terror and honour
        of life beyond the grave...
To pronounce your name now
        means death.

Song of the Blind

Don't take yourself by the hand...
Don't take yourself off beyond the river...
Don't point the finger at yourself...
Don't tell a tale about yourself...
You walk and walk – and will stumble.

[1963]

She Speaks

I was a certain forbidden book,
for which you burned with a black passion.
I was a boy-hunter
and you were my hawk.
We played so many roles

and even destruction could not save us.
You held me in a black pit.
I carried your head on a platter.
So, you were my Orpheus,
my Olophern and my John the Baptist,
I cherished my harsh dream
and I did not realise we were beautiful.
Let the curtain rise
and the holy oak burn again...
Hunter, Tsarevich, Hippolytus –
you will come out of the night forest.

....

You bang harder and more insistently
on the invisible door every time.
But what is coming to pass now
is even more terrible and shameful.
Midnight itself cannot comprehend
who is in love with whom, who the poet is,
and that I didn't perish, but split in two –
and this world cannot take the two of us.

The Big Confession

Introduction

Allow me to conceal everything: my sex, height,
colour of skin, religion, even my date of birth –
in other words everything that can be concealed.
But I cannot conceal – the lack of talent
and something else, the rest you can conceal
for your own health.

1.

24 August 1963

They say that some fragments of an old letter
have been found in a building that was once
bombed and has been reconstructed.
You might think it was a trivial matter,
however on checking it was proved right.
The handwriting seemed familiar to everyone,
and everyone seemed to think that something
like that and a whole lot of similar devilry,
had happened in their life,

(Dictate, dictate, I will listen to you
on my knees – I am sick too with an inconsolable
thirst – but we'll conceal that.)
X wanted to make a story out of it,
but everyone sided up against him.

2.

Enough of these works,
signed by someone else's hand,
all this will be ours and about us.
But what is 'ours'? And what's it about?
Now listen.

From the Confession

This tenderness was not the same
as that which a certain poet,
at the beginning of the century,
called real and, for some reason, timid. No,
not at all, it resounded like the first waterfall,
crunched like a crust of blue ice,
and entreated with the voice of a swan,
and went mad before our very eyes.

3.

Everything was decorous and worthy:
it was the Twentieth Century, Moscow, the beginning of spring,
friends and books, and sunsets in the window.
. . . .
We should have become enemies then and there,
sensing that something was wrong,
but somehow we did not realise it,
and time slipped by. Rubbish.
The world has seen more momentous things than this.
Anyway, I don't know. Did not the wind
blow from hell, or did we suddenly
feel its magic gusts?
It's all over. The ship is sinking,
the masks are off – and you and I are prisoners.
I still hear the fresh call of liberty,
it seems to me that freedom is my lot,
and 'those living waters' can be sensed,
by which the young Pushkin once sang.

4.

I remember we were both prepared
to suffer the unexpected gifts of Fate
as required and with a calm stoicism,
and perhaps with a little sarcasm.
But we were afraid of dying of tenderness
for each other – and this fear grew

and gradually filled the space
which so invincibly and with such
mourning lay between us...
which in fact it never came
into our heads to cut through.
Alongside, Phaedra spoke loudly
her unlikely confessions
to us, proud people who were already tired;
and Dante's Francesca who, 'read no more that day',
worried about her status as first lady.
I understand how complicated this all is,
but, still, try to survive.

5.

That was when the disaster happened to you.
The disaster happened – you had seen it coming.
Now you know that there is nothing on earth
that you can compare it to, or quench
that thirst that comes once a century,
perhaps even rarer, my poor friend.
Not with the winds of the free oceans,
not with the scents of tropical forests,
not with gold, nor vodka in the tavern,
not with the skipper's extra strong brandy,
not with music even when it becomes
heavenly and carries us up on high,
not even with that blessed memory
of the first unconscious love,
not with that which people call fame,
for which another would be ready to die.
You and I alone know the secret
of how to quench its thirst, but we will not tell
under evil torture, even to each other,
especially not to each other. Hush!

[1962–1963]

From the Big Confession

I came into this profession
for a multitude of crimes.
I was a traitor to the living
and faithful only to a shadow.

*　　　*　　　*　　　*

We have poisoned each other to the extent
that we could perish at any time.
We call our incomparable heaven
a black, humiliating disease.
Everything in it led to a crime,
which, God be merciful and forgive,
was the crossing of two forbidden paths
in defiance of the supreme patience.
We bear it like the chains of a holy man,
and look into it as into the waters of hell.
The most terrifying thing is that two wonderful books
will arise and tell everyone everything.

[1963]

LONG POEMS

By the Sea Shore

1.

Bays broke up the low shore,
all the sails had run off to the sea,
and I used to dry my salt-crusted hair
a couple of miles from land on a flat rock.
A green fish swam to me,
a white seagull flew to me.
I was daring, cruel and happy,
and had no idea that this was happiness.
I buried my check dress in the sand
lest the wind should blow it away, or a tramp
carry it off, and I swam far out to sea
and lay on the dark, warm waves.
As I returned, from the east
the lighthouse would already beam its alternating light.
A monk at the gates of the Chersonese
would say: 'Why are you wandering at night?'
The locals knew – I divine water,
and if they were digging a new well
they called me to find the spot
and save the men wasted work.
I used to gather French bullets,
like one gathers mushrooms or bilberries,
and brought home in my skirt
the rusted splinters of heavy shells,
and I spoke crossly to my sister:
'When I become empress
I will build six battleships
and six gunboats,
to protect my bays
right down to Cape Fiolent.'
In the evening I prayed
by my bed to the dark ikon
that the hail would not beat down the cherries,
that the fat fish would be caught,
and that a crafty tramp
would not notice the check dress.

I used to be friends with the fishermen,
and when the rain pelted down I often sat
with them under an upturned boat.
I heard about the sea, and remembered,
secretly believing every word.
The fishermen became used to me.
If I was not on the quay
the chief would send a girl for me,
and she shouted: 'Our men are back!
Tonight we shall fry the flatfish.'

The tall boy was grey-eyed,
half a year younger than me.
He brought me white roses,
white muscat roses,
and asked gently: 'Can I
sit with you on the rocks?'
I laughed, 'Why do I need roses
with their sharp thorns?' He asked,
'What can I do then,
if I am so in love with you?'
I got annoyed: 'Stupid!
What are you?' I asked, 'A prince?'
This was the grey-eyed boy,
half a year younger than me.
'I want to marry you,'
he said, 'soon I will be grown up
and will go with you to the north...'
The tall boy cried
because I did not want the roses,
did not want to go to the north.
I comforted him badly:
'Think, I will be empress,
why should I need such a husband?'
'Well then, I will become a monk,'
he said, 'near to you in the Chersonese.'
'No, don't bother. The only thing
monks do is die.
If you go there they are always burying someone —
and the others don't mourn him.'
The boy went away without a farewell.

He took the muscat roses
and I let him go.
I did not say 'Stay with me.'
The secret parting pain
cried out like a white seagull
over the grey, wormwood steppe,
over desert, dead Korsun.

2.

Bays broke up the low shore,
a smoky sun fell into the sea.
The gipsy woman came out of her cave,
beckoned me to her with her finger:
'My beauty, why do you walk around barefoot?
Soon you will be happy and rich.
Expect a noble guest before Easter,
you will greet the noble guest;
not with your beauty, not with your love,
but with your song alone will you entice the guest.'
I gave the gipsy a little chain
and a small gold christening cross.
I thought joyfully: 'Look, my darling
has given me the first news of himself.'
But out of anxiety I stopped
loving all my bays and caves.
I did not scare the viper in the reeds,
I did not bring crabs for supper.
I used to walk along the gully to the south
beyond the vineyard to the stone quarry –
it wasn't a short way.
It often happened that the owner
of the new farm waved to me,
called me from afar: 'Why don't you ever come in?
Everybody says you bring good luck.'
I would answer: 'Only horseshoes,
and the new moon that looks
into your eyes from the right are bringers of luck.'
I did not like to go indoors.
Dry winds blew from the east,
large stars fell from the sky.

270

In the lower church services were held
for the sailors who had gone to sea.
Jellyfish floated into the bay,
like stars fallen during the night
they gleamed blue deep underwater.
How the cranes called 'Coorlee' in the sky,
how the cicadas chattered restlessly,
how the soldier's wife sang of grief,
my keen ear remembered it all.
Only I knew no song
to make my prince stay with me.
I began to dream often of a girl
wearing thin bracelets and a short dress,
with a white reed-pipe in her cool hands.
She sits calmly, looks long,
will not ask about my sorrow,
and will not speak of her sorrow
only tenderly strokes my shoulder.
How will the prince recognise me?
Surely he remembers my features?
Who will point him out our old house?
Our house is well off the road.

Autumn changed to rainy winter,
wind blew through the window in the white room,
ivy hung on the low garden wall.
Strange dogs came to my yard,
howled under my window till dawn.
It was a hard time for the heart.
I whispered as I looked at the door:
'Oh God, we will rule wisely,
and build great churches by the sea,
and tall lighthouses.
We will take care of water and land,
we will not hurt a soul.'

3.

The dark sea suddenly became kinder,
the swallows returned to their nests,
and the earth turned red with poppies,

and it was good again by the sea shore.
Summer came in one night –
so we did not even glimpse spring.
I was no longer afraid
that my new fate might never come.
On the evening of Palm Sunday
as I came out of church I said to my sister:
'For you, my candle and my rosary,
our Bible I leave at home.
Easter will be here in a week,
it is high time that I got ready –
no doubt the prince is on his way by now –
he will come for me by sea.'
My sister wondered at my words in silence,
just sighed, no doubt remembered
the words of the gipsy by the cave,
'Will he bring you a necklace,
and rings set with blue stones?'
'No,' I said, 'We do not know what
gift he is preparing for me.'
My sister and I were twins,
and we were so alike
that when we were small our mother
could only recognise us by our birthmarks.
My sister could not walk from childhood,
she lay like a wax doll;
she was never cross with anyone
and she used to embroider a holy cloth.
Even in her sleep, she raved on about her work:
I heard her whispering:
'The Virgin's cloak will be blue,
O God, I can't find any pearls
for John the Apostle's tears.'
The small yard was overgrown with goose-grass and mint,
the little donkey nibbled the grass by the wicket gate.
On a long armchair
lay Lena with her arms outstretched,
always worrying about her work –
on such a holiday it is a sin to work.
The salt wind from the Chersonese
brought us the Easter bells,
each blow echoed in my heart,

coursed with my blood through the veins.
'Lena, darling Lena,' I said to my sister,
'I am going to the shore now.
If the prince comes for me
show him the way.
Let him catch me up in the steppe:
today I want to go down to the sea.'
'Where did you hear the song,
the song which will entice the prince?'
My sister asked with half-opened eyes,
'You don't even go into the town,
and here they don't sing such songs.'
I bent close up to her ear
and whispered, 'I'll tell you, Lena,
I thought up the song myself,
it's the best song in the world.'
She did not believe me, and she kept
reproachfully silent for a long time.

4.

The sun lay at the bottom of the well,
scolopendras basked on the stones,
and tumbleweed ran riot
like a hunchback clown cavorting,
and the high-soaring sky
was blue like the Virgin's cloak –
it was never like this before.
From midday light sailing ships chased each other,
many lazy white sails crowded
round Constantine battery –
wind obviously favourable now.
I walked slowly back along the bay to the cape,
to the black, shattered, sharp cliffs
foam-covered when the surf comes in,
and repeated my new song.
I knew: whoever the prince is with
he will hear my voice and be moved.
So, like a gift from God,
each word was dear to me.
The first boat did not sail, it flew,

and the second caught it up
while the others were hardly visible.
I don't remember how I lay by the water,
I don't know how I dozed off then.
Suddenly I woke: I saw a sail
flapping nearby. In front of me
a huge old man standing up to his waist
in the clear water, scrabbles with his hands
in the deep cracks of the shore cliffs,
and hoarse-voiced, calls for help.
Loudly I began to repeat the prayer
I was taught when young
to ward off terror from my dreams,
to ward off evil from my house.
I could only say: 'You are the Saviour!'
I looked – the old man carried something white in his arms –
my heart froze.
He carried out the man who sailed
the most joyful and winged sailing ship,
and placed him on the dark rocks.

For a long time I did not dare trust myself,
I bit my fingers to wake up:
my beautiful, tender prince
lay quietly and looked at the sky.
Those eyes, greener than the sea,
darker than our cypresses,
I saw them fade...
Better for me to have been born blind.
He groaned and shouted inarticulately:
'Swallow, O swallow. What agony!'
Perhaps he saw me as a bird.

I returned home at dusk.
It was quiet in the dark room.
A thin, tiny crimson flame
stood high over the ikon lamp.
'The prince did not come for you,'
Lena said when she heard footsteps.
'I waited for him till vespers,
and sent the children down to the harbour.'

'He will never come for me,
he will never return, Lena,
my prince died today.'
My sister crossed herself again and again.
She turned her face to the wall and was silent.
In my heart I knew Lena was crying.

I heard that they sang for the prince:
'Christ is risen from the dead' –
and the round church
shone with an ineffable light.

[1914]

The Way of All the Earth

1.

I will force my way
through Januarys and Julys
through a hail of bullets,
pushing aside the years.
No one will see my wound,
no one will hear my screams.
I, the Kitezh woman,
have been called home.
One hundred thousand birch trees
pursued me.
The frost flowed
in a glass wall.
The charred warehouse
lay by the burnt out fires.
'Here's my pass, comrade,
let me through round the back.'
And the soldier calmly
pulls back his bayonet.
The island emerged
so fine and burnished.
And the red clay,
and the apple orchard were there...
O, Salve Regina!
The sunset flares.
The little path climbed
steeply, tremblingly.

I need someone's hand
to hold here...
But I don't listen to the groans
of the hoarse barrel organ.
The Kitezh woman heard
the wrong chimes.

2.

Trenches, trenches —
you'll get lost in them!
The old Europe
is in rags,
where, in a cloud of smoke,
the towns are burning,
and now the ridges
of the Crimea are darkening.
With me I lead a flock
of women mourners.
O the blue cloak
of my silent land...
I stand over a dead Medusa
jellyfish, my mind at odds with itself.
Here I met the Muse
and made her my vow.
But she laughs loudly,
doesn't believe me: 'What, you?'
Fragrant April
flows in dew.
Fame's high threshold
is here already,
but a cunning voice
forewarned me:
'You will return here,
return many times,
and you will again strike
the resistance of the diamond.
Better go past,
better go back,
cursed and praised,
to your father's garden.'

3.

Mist thickens
in the evening.
Let Hoffman come with me
as far as the corner.
He knows the stifled
scream that echoes,
and whose double has
dodged into the sidestreet.
It's no joke
that for twenty five years
I have continually seen
before me this ghastly silhouette.
'So it's on the right is it?
Just round the corner?
Thanks.' A ditch,
and a small house.
I did not know the moon
was so completely involved.
It rushed down
the trellis ladder,
and calmly walks around
the abandoned house,
where the night on its way out
looked over the round table
at the splinters of
shattered mirrors,
and a murdered man
slept on a mound of darkness.

4.

There is a lofty power
of purest sound,
as though parting
had a thoroughly good time.
Familiar buildings
look out from death –
and a meeting would
be a hundred times sadder

than everything that had ever
happened to me...
I walk home through
the crucified city.

5.

The cherry blossom stole
past like a dream.
Somebody said 'Tsushima!'
on the telephone.
Quickly, quickly –
time is running out:
the *Varyag* and the *Koreyets* warships
have gone off to the East...
There the old agony
of the swallow throngs,
and farther away
Fort Shabrol looms
like a smashed crypt
of the last century,
where an old cripple
went deaf and blind.
Stern, sullen
Boers guard it
with rifles at the ready.
'Get back! Back!'

6.

I waited a long time
for the great winter to come,
and put it on
like a white cowl.
And I sit calmly
on the light sledge.
I'll return to you men and women
of Kitezh before nightfall.
There's one crossing
by the old ferry stage.

Neither brother, nor neighbour
nor bridegroom
will accompany me,
the Kitezh woman –
just the conifer's twig,
and a sunlit poem,
dropped by a beggar
and picked up by me...
Lay me to rest
in my last dwelling place.

[Fountain House, March 1940]

Requiem: *Poems 1935-1940*

No, not under a foreign sky,
not under the shelter of alien wings –
I was with my people then,
there where my people were doomed to be.
          1961

Instead of a Foreword

During the terrible years of the Yezhov Terror I spent seventeen months in the prison queues in Leningrad. One day someone 'identified' me. Then a woman with lips blue with cold who was standing behind me, and of course had never heard of my name, came out of the numbness which affected us all and whispered in my ear – (we all spoke in whispers there):
     'Could you describe this?'
     I said, 'I can!'
     Then something resembling a smile slipped over what had once been her face.

[1 April 1957]

Dedication

The mountains bend before this grief,
the great river does not flow,
but the prison locks are strong,
and behind them the convict-holes,
and the anguish of death.
Someone basks in the sunset,
for someone the fresh wind blows.
We don't know, we are the same everywhere.
We only hear the repellent clank of keys,
the heavy steps of the soldiers.
We rose as though to early mass,
and went through the savage capital.
We used to meet each other there, more lifeless than the dead,
the sun lower, the Neva mistier,
but hope still sings in the distance.

Condemned...The sudden rush of tears.
One woman, already isolated from everyone else,
as though her life had been wrenched from her heart,
as though she had been smashed flat on her back,
she walks on...staggers...alone...
Where now are the captive companions
of my two hellish years?
What do they see in the Siberian blizzard,
what comes to them in the moon's circle?
I send them my farewell greeting.

[March 1940]

Introduction

It was a time when only the dead
smiled, happy in their peace.
And Leningrad dangled like a useless appendage
at the side of its prisons.
A time when, out of their minds with suffering,
the convicted walked in regiments,
and the steam whistles sang
their short parting song.
Stars of death stood over us
and innocent Russia squirmed
under the bloody boots,
under the wheels of Black Marias.

I.

They took you away at dawn.
I walked after you as though you were being carried out
        in a coffin.
The children were crying in the dark room,
the candle guttered by the ikon-stand.
The cold of the ikon on your lips.
Death sweat on your brow. I will not forget!
I will howl by the Kremlin towers
like the Streltsy wives.

282

II.

The quiet Don flows quietly.
The yellow moon goes into the house,

goes in with its cap askew.
The yellow moon sees the shadow.

This woman is sick,
this woman is alone,

husband in the grave, son in prison,
pray for me.

III.

No, this is not me – someone else suffers.
I couldn't stand this: let black drapes
cover what happened,
and let them take away the lamps...
   Night.

IV.

If I could show your former ironic self,
that once carefree sinner of Tsarskoye Selo,
so popular in your circle of friends,
how your life will turn out:
you will stand outside the Crosses Prison
three hundredth in the line with your prison parcel,
and burn through the new-year ice
with your hot tears.
There the prison poplar sways
in silence. How many
innocent lives are ending there...

V.

For seventeen months I have been screaming,
calling you home.
I flung myself at the executioner's feet.
You are my son and my terror.
Everything is confused for ever,
and I can no longer tell
beast from man,
How long must I wait for the execution?
There are only the dusty flowers,
the clank of censers, and tracks
leading somewhere to nowhere.
An enormous star
looks me straight in the eye
and threatens swift destruction.

[1939]

VI.

Weightless weeks fly by.
I will never grasp what happened.
How the white nights looked
at you, my boy, in prison,
how they look again
with the burning eye of the hawk,
they speak of your crucifixion,
they speak of death.

[1939]

VII. *Sentence*

The stone word fell
on my still beating breast.
Never mind, I was prepared,
somehow I'll come to terms with it.

Today I have much work to do:
I must finally kill my memory,
I must so my soul can turn to stone,
I must learn to live again.

Or else...The hot summer rustle,
like holiday time outside my window.
I have felt this coming for a long time,
this bright day and the deserted house.

[Summer 1939]

VIII. *To Death*

You will come anyway – so why not now?
I am waiting for you – it's very difficult for me.
I have put out the light and opened the door
to you so simple and wonderful.
Assume any shape you like,
burst in as the poison'd shot of slander,
or creep up like a skilled burglar with a lead pipe,
or poison me with typhus vapours,
or come with a denunciation invented by you
and known *ad nauseam* to everyone,
so that I may see the peak of the blue cap
and the janitor's fear-whitened face.
I don't care now. The Yenisey rolls on,
the Pole star shines.
And the blue lustre of beloved eyes
is clouded by the final horror.

[19 August 1939]

IX.

Already madness has covered
half my soul with its wing,
and gives me strong liquor to drink,
and lures me to the black valley.

I realised that I must
hand victory to it,
as I listened to my delirium,
already alien to me.

It will not allow me to take
anything away with me,
(however I beseech it,
however I pester it with prayer):

not the terrible eyes of my son,
the rock-like suffering,
not the night when the storm came,
not the prison visiting hour,

nor the sweet coolness of hands,
nor the uproar of the lime trees' shadows,
nor the distant light sound —
the words of last comfort.

[4 May 1940]

X.   *Crucifixion*

'Weep not for Me, Mother,
when thou lookest in the grave.'

1.

The angels' choir glorified the great hour,
the heavens melted in flames.
He said to His Father: 'Why hast Thou forsaken Me?'
and to His Mother: 'Oh, weep not for Me...'

2.

Mary Magdalene smote her breast and wept,
the disciple whom He loved turned to stone,
but where the Mother stood in silence
nobody even dared look.

[1940–1943]

Epilogue

1.

I found out how faces droop,
how terror looks out from under the eyelids,
how suffering carves on cheeks
hard pages of cuneiform,
how curls ash-blonde and black
turn silver overnight.
A smile fades on submissive lips,
fear trembles in a dry laugh.
I pray not for myself alone,
but for everyone who stood with me
in the cruel cold, in the July heat,
under the blinded, red wall.

2.

The hour of remembrance has drawn close again.
I see you, hear you, feel you:

the one they could hardly get to the window,
the one who no longer walks on this earth,

the one who shook her beautiful head,
and said: 'Coming here is like coming home.'

I would like to name them all but they took away
the list and there's no way of finding them.

For them I have woven a wide shroud
from the humble words I heard among them.

I remember them always, everywhere,
I will never forget them, whatever comes.

And if they gag my tormented mouth
with which one hundred million people cry,

then let them also remember me
on the eve of my remembrance day.

If they ever think of building
a memorial to me in this country,

I consent to be so honoured,
only with this condition: not to build it

near the sea where I was born:
my last tie with the sea is broken,

nor in the Tsar's Garden by the hallowed stump
where an inconsolable shadow seeks me,

but here, where I stood three hundred hours
and they never unbolted the door for me.

Since even in blessed death I am terrified
that I will forget the thundering of Black Marias,

forget how the hateful door slammed,
how an old woman howled like a wounded beast.

Let the melting snow stream
like tears from my bronze eyelids,

let the prison dove call in the distance
and the boats go quietly on the Neva.

[March 1940]

POEM WITHOUT A HERO

Triptych

(1940-1962)

LENINGRAD – TASHKENT – MOSCOW

DEUS CONSERVAT OMNIA
Motto on the crest of Fountain House

INSTEAD OF A FOREWORD

Some are no more, others are far away.

It came to me for the first time in the night of the 27th December 1940 when I was living in Fountain House. Already that autumn it had sent as a messenger one small fragment ('You came into Russia from nowhere').

I didn't call it. I didn't even expect it that cold, dark day of my last Leningrad winter.

Its appearance was preceded by a few small and insignificant facts which I cannot bring myself to call events.

That night I wrote two fragments of the first part ('1913' and 'Dedication'). At the beginning of January I almost surprised myself by writing 'Tails' and in Tashkent, in two sittings, I wrote 'Epilogue' which became the third part of the poem, and made a few important additions to the two earlier parts.

I dedicate this poem to the memory of the people who first heard it, my friends and fellow-citizens who perished in the siege of Leningrad. I hear their voices and remember them when I read the poem aloud, and this secret chorus has become for ever the justification of the poem for me.

[Tashkent, 8 April 1943]

FIRST DEDICATION
27 December 1940

...and since I have run out of paper
I write on your rough draft.
And look, a word which is not mine shows through
and, as a snowflake did then upon a palm
melts trustingly and without rebuke.
The dark eyelashes of Antinoüs
lifted suddenly – and there was green smoke,
and a familiar breeze awoke...
Is it not the sea?
                    No it is only fir trees
around a grave and in the foam boiling
ever closer and closer...
                        Marche funèbre
                            Chopin...

[Fountain House, night of 27 December 1940]

SECOND DEDICATION
To O.A.G-S.

Is it you Confuser Psyche,
waving a black-and-white fan,
leaning over me,
who want to tell me a secret
that you have already crossed the Lethe
and are breathing in another spring?
Don't dictate to me, I myself hear:
a warm shower hitting the roof,
a soft whisper in the ivy.
Some little thing has decided to live,
turned green and fluffy, tries
to dazzle tomorrow in a new cloak.
I sleep –
        it alone is over me,
which is called spring by other people
and which I call solitude.

290

I sleep – I dream of our young days,
that cup that passed Him by;
once awake, if you wish,
I shall give it to you for a memory
like a clean flame in a clay lamp
or a snowdrop in the grave's ditch.

[Fountain House, 25 May 1945]

THIRD AND LAST

> *Once on an Epiphany evening*
> Zhukovsky

Enough of my turning icy from terror,
it's better to call forth the Bach Chaconne,
and after it a man will enter.
He won't become my dear husband
but together we shall earn the right
to confuse the Twentieth Century.
It happened by chance that I took him in:
he who was endowed with a secret,
and with whom there is a bitter fate.
He comes to see me in the palace on the Fontanka
late in the misty night
to drink the New Year wine.
He will remember the Epiphany eve,
the maple at the window, the wedding candles
and the poem's deathly flight...
But he will not bring me the first spray of lilac,
a ring, nor the sweetness of prayers.
He will bring me – destruction.

[5 January 1956]
(Le Jour des Rois)

K

INTRODUCTION

FROM THE YEAR NINETEEN FORTY
I LOOK DOWN ON EVERYTHING AS FROM A TOWER.
AS IF SAYING GOODBYE AGAIN
TO WHAT I SAID FAREWELL TO LONG AGO,
AS IF I HAD CROSSED MYSELF
AND AM GOING DOWN UNDER THE DARK VAULTS...

[Leningrad under siege,
25 August 1941]

PART ONE

Nineteen Thirteen

A Petersburg Tale
CHAPTER ONE

> *Di rider finirai*
> *Pria dell'Aurora*
>> Don Giovanni

> *The New Year holiday lingers luxuriously,*
> *the stems of New Year roses are damp.*
>> Rosary

> *We will not tell fortunes with Tatiana...*
>> Onegin

> *In my hot youth when George the Third was King*
>> Don Juan

New Year's Eve. Fountain House. Instead of the expected person
the shades of 1913 come to the author under the guise of
mummers. A white hall of mirrors. A lyrical interlude – 'the guest
from the future'. Masquerade. Poet. Ghost.

I have lit my sacred candles
so that this evening should be bright,
and with you who have not come to me
I meet the year nineteen forty-one.
But...
The Lord's strength be with us!
The flame has sunk in the crystal
and 'the wine burns like poison'.
These are the splashes of a tough conversation,
when deliriums rise again
and clocks still don't strike...
My anxiety has no limit,
I myself, like a shadow on the threshold
watch over my last comfort.
I hear a long ring of the bell,
and I feel a damp chill,
I turn to stone, am cold, burn...
And as though remembering something turn
in profile speaking
in a soft voice:
'You have come to the wrong place: Venice of the Doges
is over there...Today you will have to leave
your croziers, cloaks, masks and crowns
in the hall.
I've decided to glorify you now
my New Year revellers!'
This one as Faust, this one as Don Juan,
one as Dapertutto, one as John the Baptist,
the most modest as the Northern Glahn,
or as the murderer Dorian,
and all whisper to their Dianas
the same old stories.
For them the walls separated,
the lights flashed, the sirens screeched
and the ceiling bulged like a dome.
I am not one who fears publicity...
What's the state of Hamlet's garters to me?
or the whirl of Salome's dance,
or the pacing of the Man in the Iron Mask?
I myself am more of iron than those...
Whose turn is it to be frightened,

to reel away, to recoil, to surrender,
and to pray for forgiveness for sins long past?
Everything is clear:
                    for whom have they come if not for me?
Dinner has not been prepared here for them,
and we don't share the same path.
He hid his tail under his frock coat...
How lame yet elegant he is...
However...
I hope you haven't dared to bring
the Lord of Darkness here?
Is this a skull or a face or a mask,
the expression of evil pain
that only Goya could dare paint?
The most stinking sinner
is grace incarnate
before everyone's clown, this artist at mocking.
If we are to be merry, well let's be merry!
Only how could it have happened
that I alone of them am alive?
Tomorrow the morning will wake me
and nobody will condemn me
and the blue beyond the window pane
will laugh in my face.
But I am afraid: I shall enter the hall
without taking off my lace shawl,
I shall smile at everyone and fall silent.
I never again want to meet
that person that I once was,
in a necklace of black agate
until the valley of the Last Judgement.
Are not the last times close?
I forgot your lessons,
false prophets and rhetoricians,
but you didn't forget me –
as the future matures in the past
so the past decays in the future –
terrible festival of dead leaves.

W	There is the sound of steps, over the gleaming parquet floor,
H	of those who are not here.
I	The blue cigar smoke
T	and in all the mirrors the reflection of a man
E	who did not appear
	and could not penetrate into the hall.
H	He is neither better nor worse than others,
A	however he does not smell of the Lethe's chill,
L	and there is warmth in his hand.
L	Will he really come to me,
	turning left after the bridge?
	The guest from the future!

...Since childhood I have feared mummers,
it always seemed to me
that some superfluous shadow
had intruded itself among them
'faceless, nameless'...
                    Let us begin the festivities
on this triumphal New Year's day!
I will not begin to tell the world
my midnight tales of Hoffman.
I would have asked others instead...
                    Stop!
your name is not on the lists
of Cagliostros, magi and Lysiscas,
dressed in the motley vulgarity
of a striped mile-post.
You are the same age as the Mamre oak,
who eternally talks and listens to the moon.
Your feigned groans will not deceive us.
Hammurabis, Lycurgus's, Solons,
should learn to write
laws of iron from you.
He has a strange temperament.
He does not wait for gout and glory
to place him, before his time
in luxurious jubilee chairs.
Instead he carries his triumph
through flowering heather and deserts.

And he is guilty of nothing, not of this,
not of that, and not of any other thing...
Sins, on the whole, don't importune poets:
they must dance before the Ark of the Covenant
or else disappear. But what's the point?
Their poems are the authority on this.
The cock's crow only comes to us in dreams,
outside the window the fog billows on the Neva,
the night is bottomless,
the black mass in Petersburg drags on and on...
No star can be seen through the narrow windows.
The disaster is imminent,
but the masked chatter is
thoughtless, spicy, shameless.
A shout:
   'Lead to the front stage!'
Don't be upset: he will certainly come out
now to replace the lanky man,
and will sing of sacred vengeance...
Why do you all rush off together?
as though each of you had found a bride,
leaving me in the darkness
eye to eye with the black frame,
out of which looks that hour
as yet unmourned,
which became the most bitter drama.

This is not all happening in a moment.
I hear a whisper like a single musical phrase:
'Farewell! It's time!
I will leave you alive,
however you will be my widow,
you are my little dove, my sun, my sister!'
Two shadows merged on the landing...
And then, from the steps of a shallow staircase:
a scream: 'Don't do it!' And a pure voice
in the distance: 'I am ready for death.'

(The torches go out, the ceiling lowers. The white hall of mirrors
again becomes the room of the author. Words from the dark-
ness:)

There is no death, everyone knows that,
to keep repeating that is boring,
but what is there, let them tell me.
Who knocks?
             We let everyone in, didn't we,
is this the guest from the wrong side of the mirror
or something which just flashed in the window?
Is the young moon playing a joke,
or is somebody really standing once again
between the stove and that cupboard?
Eyes open, forehead pale...
This means that gravestones are crumbling,
this means that granite is softer than wax...
Rubbish, rubbish, rubbish! From such rubbish
I will go grey soon,
or become someone completely different.
Why are you beckoning me?

I'd give up my peace after death
for one moment of it now.

ACROSS THE LANDING
(Intermezzo)

'I assure you there's nothing new...'
'You are a child, signor Casanova...'
'At St Isaac's about six...'
'Somehow we'll get there through the fog,
from there we've still got to drop in at the Stray Dog.'
'Where are you going from here?'
                    'God knows!'
Sancho Panzas and Don Quixotes,
and alas, Lots from Sodom
try the deadly drinks.

297

Aphrodites have risen from the foam,
Helens have moved in the mirrors,
and the time of madness approaches.
Again from the Fontanka Grotto,
where love sighs drowsily,
someone with shaggy red hair
dragged the goat-legged nymph
through the ghostly gates.
The head of Madame Lamballe
is more elegant and aristocratic
than all the others,
although seeing nothing, hearing nothing,
not swearing, not praying, not even breathing.
But you, meek and beautiful,
who dance the goat dance,
again coo gently:
'Que me veut mon Prince Carnival?'

At the same time in the depth of the hall, of the stage, of hell or on the height of Goethe's Brocken, *She* herself appears (or perhaps her shadow).

She ran, as though from a black-figure vase
to the azure wave,
so ceremoniously naked.
Her boots stamp like little hooves,
her earrings ring like tiny sleighbells,
her evil little horns in pale curls,
drunk with the cursed dance.
You Ivanushka, simpleton of the old tale
entering behind her without your mask
in overcoat and helmet,
what tortures you today?
How much bitterness there is in each word you say,
how much gloom in your love,
and why does this trickle of blood
irritate the petal of your cheek?

298

CHAPTER TWO

Or do you see at your knees that man still alive,
who preferred white death to being your captive.
Voice of Memory 1913

The heroine's bedroom. A wax candle burns. Over the bed there
are three portraits of the mistress of the house in different roles.
On the right she is the Goat-legged Nymph, in the middle the
Confuser, on the left the portrait is in shadow. To some it seems
that it is Columbine, to others Donna Anna (from 'The Steps of
the Commendatore'). Outside the garret window the stage hands
in black face play snowballs. Snowstorm. New Year's Eve. The
Confuser comes alive, comes down from the portrait and she
seems to hear a voice that reads:

Fling open the satin-lined fur coat!
Don't be angry with me, because I've drunk
from this chalice, too, my little dove.
I am sentencing myself not you.
Retribution comes anyway.
You see, there beyond the grainy snowstorm
Meyerhold's stage hands in black face stir
and bustle once more.
And round about the old city Peter,
which wore down the people,
(as the people used to say then),
with strings of flour carts, manes, harnesses,
kitschy tea-roses,
under the cloud of crows' wings.
Pavlova, our ineffable swan, flies over
the stage of the Mariinsky Theatre,
smiling artificially,
while a snob who's come in late cracks witticisms.
The orchestra sounds as if it's from another world
somewhere a shadow of something flashed,
and a fever ran through the rows of seats
like a premonition of dawn.
And again the familiar voice of Chaliapin,
like an echo of thunder in the mountains –
is it not our final triumph?

It fills the heart with trembling,
and rushes into the most remote corners
of the country that nurtured it.
Bluish white snow covers the branches.
The corridor of the Twelve Colleges
is endless, ringing and straight,
(anything may happen here it seems,
but it will stubbornly turn up in the dreams
of those who walk through it).
The dénouement is so close it's absurd;
and the mask of Petrushka peeps from behind the curtains,
the coachmen dance around the bonfires,
the black and yellow flag is flying over the palace,
everything which is needed is already in place:
the last act is blowing up from the Summer Garden.
A ghost from the hell of Tsushima is there,
and a drunken sailor sings.
How splendidly the runners ring,
and the goatskin rug drags...
Pass, shadows! He is there alone.
On the wall is the sharp profile,
of a Mephistopheles or Gabriel,
my beauty, your paladin.
The demon, smiled at by Tamara,
hides such charms
in his terrible smoky face.
In the stranger everything is mysterious,
flesh that almost became spirit
and an antique curl over the ear.
Was it he who sent that black rose in the wine glass,
across the crowded hall
or was this all a dream?
Did he steal into the accursed house
with a dead heart and dead glance
and meet up with the Commendatore?
His words have revealed to us
how you were in a new space,
how you were outside time,
in that polar crystal ice,
in the amber Northern Lights,
there by the mouth of the Lethe-Neva.

You vanished from the portrait
and the empty frame will wait
for you on the wall till dawn.
Your fate is to dance without a partner.
I am ready to accept for myself
the role of Greek chorus.

(There are crimson patches on your cheeks,
you should go back again into the canvas.
Tonight is one of those nights
in which you have to settle the bill...
and this narcotic stupor
is harder to overcome than death.)

...You came into Russia from nowhere,
O my Columbine of the 1910s:
Why is your look so piercing, and so troubled?
O my blonde starlet,
actress, Petersburg doll.
You are one of my doubles.
You must add this
to your other titles. O friend of the poets,
I am the heir to your fame.
I see the court skeletons dance
to the music of the wonderful maestro,
the wild Leningrad wind
in the shadow of the protected cedar...
The candles burn down,
shoulders long for kisses under the bridal veil.
The church resounds with the wedding march.
The mountains of Parma violets in April,
and a meeting in the Maltese chapel,
are like a curse in your breast.
Is it a vision of the golden age,
or a black crime
in the threatening chaos of the distant past?
Answer me at once,
is it possible you really lived,
and your dazzling feet trod
the wooden pavements of our squares?

A house more motley than a carnival caravan,
chipped Cupids
protect the altar of Venus.
Your songbirds flew free.
You arranged your bedroom like a summerhouse.
The happy country bumpkin would not recognise
his girl neighbour.
The spiral staircase is hidden in the walls,
and there are ikons of saints on those pale blue walls,
but these things are half-stolen...
Surrounded by flowers, like Botticelli's Primavera,
you received your friends in bed,
and the Pierrot of the Dragoons suffered.
He is the most superstitious of all those in love with you
and he has the smile of a victim of the evening.
You are to him as a magnet to steel.
Turning pale, he watches through his tears,
how you are handed roses,
and how his enemy is famous.
I did not see your husband,
as I pressed my face against the cold glass of the window...
There it is, the striking of the fortress clock...
Do not be afraid — I don't put the crosses on houses,
come boldly out to meet me,
your horoscope has been cast long ago.

CHAPTER THREE

Under the arch on Galernaya Street
A. Akhmatova

We will meet again in Petersburg
as if we had buried the sun there
O. Mandelstam

It was the last year...
M. Lozinsky

Petersburg in 1913. A lyrical interlude: last memory in Tsarskoye Selo. The wind half remembering, half prophesying, mutters:

Christmastide was burning with bonfires
and carriages skidded off bridges
and the whole funereal city was floating
to an unknown assignation
down the Neva or against the current –
only to get away from its graves.
The arch gaped black on Galernaya Street.
The weathervane sang a shrill song in the Summer Garden
and a bright silver moon
froze over the Silver Age.
A shadow was slowly approaching
along all roads,
to all doorsteps.
The wind ripped posters off the walls,
the smoke danced Cossack dances on the roof,
and lilac smelled of the cemetery.
The city disappeared into the mist,
Dostoyevskian and possessed
and damned by Avdotya the Tsaritsa.
Peter, the old debaucher,
looked out of the darkness again
and heard the drum beat as before the execution...
In the frosty, menacing and prodigal
claustrophobia of the pre-war years
there always existed a foreboding rumble.
It was barely audible, then,
it hardly touched the hearing
and was drowned in the Neva snowdrifts.
A man raves and does not
want to recognise himself
as if in the mirror of a terrible night.
And along the legendary embankment
the real Twentieth Century approached
with 1914.

(And now home quickly
by the Cameron Gallery
into the icebound mysterious garden
where the waterfalls are silent,
where all Nine Muses will be happy for me,
as you once were.
There beyond the island, there beyond the park,
will our eyes not meet
with their former clarity?
Won't you ever again say to me
the word that conquers death
and is the solution of my life's riddle?)

FOURTH AND LAST CHAPTER

> *Love has passed and the features of death*
> *have become clear and close.*
> Vs. Knyazev

A corner of the Field of Mars. A house built at the beginning of the XIXth century by the Adamini brothers. In the bombing of 1942 it will suffer a direct hit. A high bonfire burns. The ringing of the bells from the Cathedral of the Spilt Blood is heard. In the field beyond the snowstorm the ghosts of the Winter Palace Ball. In the interval between these sounds Silence itself speaks:

Who froze still by the darkened windows,
on whose breast is the straw-coloured curl,
who has darkness before his eyes?
'Help! It is still not too late!'
Night, never were you
so frosty, so strange.
The wind is laden with Baltic salt.
The snowstorms use the Field of Mars as a ballroom,
and invisible hooves ring out...

304

The anxiety of somebody who has
not long to live is immeasurable.
He is only asking God for death
and will be forgotten for ever.
He wanders beneath the windows after midnight.
The dull light of the corner street-lamp
falls on him mercilessly –
his wait was over. A beautiful masked woman
going back from 'The Road from Damascus'
returned home – not alone!
Somebody is with her 'faceless, nameless':
he saw an unequivocal parting
through the slanting flames of the bonfire –
the buildings collapsed around him,
and in answer a fragment of crying:
'You are my little dove, my sun, my sister!
I will leave you alive
but you will be *my* widow,
and now...
                    Time to say farewell!'
There is a smell of perfume on the landing,
and the cornet of Dragoons with the poems
and with a senseless death in his heart
will ring the doorbell if he dares.
He will spend his last moment
in glorifying you.
                    Look:
not in the damned Masurian marshes,
not on the blue Carpathian heights...
He has fallen across your threshold...
May God forgive you!

(How many deaths did the poet have coming to him?
The stupid boy: he chose this one –
he could not bear the first wounds.
He did not know what threshold
he was standing on, and what prospects
the road opened out before him...)

It is I – your old conscience
  who sought out the burnt story
    and placed it on the edge of the windowsill
      in the house of the dead man
        and walked out
          on tiptoe...

AFTERWORD

EVERYTHING IS IN ORDER: THE POEM LIES
IN CHARACTERISTIC SILENCE.
BUT WHAT IF A THEME SHOULD BREAK OUT
KNOCKING ON THE WINDOW WITH A FIST?
AND FROM THE DISTANCE THIS TERRIBLE SOUND
RESPONDS TO THE CALL –
GURGLING, GROANING AND SCREECHING,
AND THE VISION OF CROSSED HANDS...

PART TWO

Tails

My future is in my past

I drink the waters of the Lethe.
My doctor's forbidden me to be depressed.
              Pushkin

The place of action is Fountain House. The time 5th January
1941. In the window the ghost of the snowy maple. The hellish
harlequinade of 1913 has only just passed by disturbing the
silence of the great silent epoch, and leaving behind it the chaos
characteristic of any festive or funeral procession – smoke of
torches, flowers on the ground, sacred souvenirs lost fore-
ver...The wind howls in the stove pipe and in this howling one
can divine fragments of *Requiem* very deeply and very cunningly
concealed. Of what appears in the mirrors – it's best not to think.

...The jasmine branch
where Dante walked and the air is empty
              N. Klyuev

I

My editor was in a bad mood,
he swore to me that he was busy and sick
and his telephone was ex-directory.
He grumbled: 'There are three themes at once!
and when you've read the last sentence
you don't know who's in love with whom,

II

who, when and why they met,
who perished and who remained alive,
and who the author is and who the hero is –
and what do these musings mean
to us today about a poet
and some swarm of ghosts or other?'

307

L

III

I answered: 'There are three of them –
the main one was dressed up like a milepost
and the other like a devil;
Their poems strove for them
so that they should reach across the centuries.
The third only lived twenty years

IV

and I'm sorry for him.' And again
word fell after word,
the music box thundered
and mysterious poison flamed
over this cracked flask
with a crooked and angry tongue of fire.

V

And in my dream it still seemed
that I was writing some libretto
and there was no respite from the music.
Really the dream – that's something else too,
'soft embalmer', Bluebird,
the ramparts of the Elsinore terraces.

VI

I was not happy myself
having heard from afar the wailing
of this hellish masquerade.
I still hoped that it would rush off
past the white hall, into the twilight
of fir branches, like grainy smoke.

VII

There's no defence against this florid stuff –
here's the old Cagliostro fooling around,
himself the most elegant Satan,
who does not share our mourning of the dead,
who does not know what conscience means
and why it exists.

VIII

It doesn't feel like a Roman
midnight carnival. A Cherubim choir
sings by the closed churches.
No one knocks at my door,
only mirror dreams of mirror,
silence guards silence.

IX

My Seventh is with me,
half dead and dumb,
its mouth tensed and open,
like the mouth of a tragic mask,
except it's daubed in black paint
and packed with dry earth.

X

...and the decades pass:
tortures, exiles, executions –
you see I cannot sing them.

XI

...

XII

...

XIII

Will I dissolve into a state anthem?
Don't give me, don't give me, don't give me
the diadem from the dead brow.
Soon I will need a lyre,
but Sophokles' not Shakespeare's.
Fate stands on the threshold.

XIV ·

That theme for me
was like a chrysanthemum crushed
on the floor when they carry the coffin.
Between memory and remembering, my friends,
it is as far as from Luga
to the land of the satin masks.

XV

The devil tempted me to rummage in the chest...
Well, how could it happen
that I am guilty of everything?
I – the quietest, I – the simple one,
Wayside Grass, White Flock...
Justify myself, but how, my friends?

XVI

You should know this: they will accuse me of plagiarism...
Am I more guilty than others?
It doesn't make any difference,
I am prepared for failure,
and I won't hide my confusion...
for the casket has a treble bottom.

XVII

But I confess I used
invisible ink,
and I write a mirror letter,
and for me there is no other way –
by a miracle I stumbled on this,
and I am not in a hurry to part with it.

XVIII

Thus an emissary from a distant age,
from El Greco's sacred dream,
explained to me completely without words,
but with just a summer smile,
that I was more forbidden to him
than all the seven deadly sins.

XIX

Then let the eyes of the unknown man
from the future age
look so boldly that he should give
me, the departing shade,
an armful of moist lilac
in the hour when this storm has passed.

310

XX

The century old enchantress
suddenly came to and wanted
to make merry. It's nothing to do with me.
She drops a lace handkerchief,
casts languid glances from behind the lines,
and shows off her eminently paintable shoulder.

XXI

I drank her in drop by drop
and possessed by a devilish,
black thirst I did not know how
to separate myself from the demonic one:
I threatened her with the Star Chamber,
and chased her to her home garret,

XXII

into the darkness under the Manfred fir trees,
and to the shore where the dead Shelley
lay looking straight into the sky,
and all the skylarks of the whole world
burst the abyss of the ether,
and George Byron carried the torch.

XXIII

But The Poem repeated stubbornly:
'I am not that English Lady,
and definitely not Clara Gazoul,
I have no genealogy at all,
apart from the sun and folklore,
and July itself brought me here.

XXIV

I shall still honour
your ambiguous glory
that's lain in the ditch for twenty years.
We will still feast together
and I will reward your evil midnight
with my royal kiss.'

[Fountain House, 3–5 January 1941, Tashkent and after]

PART THREE

Epilogue

I love you creation of Peter!
Pushkin: *Bronze Horseman*

And the deserts of the mute squares
where they executed people till dawn.
Annensky

White night of the 24th June 1942. The city is in ruins. From the Harbour to Smolny as far as the eye can see all is rased to the ground. Here and there old fires burn out. In the Sheremetev Garden the lime trees blossom and the nightingale sings. One window on the third storey (before which is the crippled maple) is blown out and behind it the black emptiness yawns. Heavy guns boom round Kronstadt, but in general it's quiet. Seven thousand kilometres away, the voice of the author speaks:

Evening tranquility wanders
with a lamp and a bunch of keys
under the roof of Fountain House.
My howl echoed in the distance
disturbing the unwakeable sleep of things
with inappropriate laughter.
The old maple that witnesses everything in the world
at sunset and at dawn,
looks into the room
and foreseeing our parting
extends its dried out black hand
to me as if to help.
But the earth rumbled underfoot
and the star watched
my not yet deserted house,
and waited for the prearranged signal...
It is somewhere there at Tobruk,
it is somewhere here behind the corner.
(You are not the first and not the last
dark listener of bright deliriums.

What vengeance are you preparing for me?
You will not drink up, only sip, a drop
of this bitterness from the very depth,
the news of this our parting.
Don't put your hand upon my head.
Unhappiness will not pass us by,
and the cuckoo will not cry cuckoo
in our burned down forests...)
Behind the barbed wire,
in the very heart of the dense taiga –
I don't know in which year –
becoming a handful of "camp dust",
becoming a story, but based on fact,
my double goes to the interrogation,
guarded by two escorts
from the 'Noseless "Maiden"'.
Isn't it miraculous
that even from here
I can hear the sound of my own voice:
I paid in cash for you,
I walked under the revolver, for exactly ten years,
looking neither left nor right,
pursued by the rustle of gaunt glory.

You, seditious, disgraced, dear
although you turned pale, dead and still,
did not become my grave.
Our parting is false:
you and I are inseparable.
My shadow is on your walls,
my reflection in the canals,
the sounds of footsteps in the halls of the Hermitage,
where my friend walked with me,
and on the old Wolf Field,
where I can weep in freedom
over the silence of my brothers' graves.
The Poem flew free, casting off
all that is said in the First Part
about love, betrayal and passion.
My city is still standing, but sewn up in a shroud.
The tombstone lids are heavy
on its sleepless eyes.

You stayed behind to perish
in the spires' reflection in the sparkling waters
and it seemed it was me
that you were pursuing.
You did not live to see the longed for messengers...
Above you is only the round dance
of your charming white nights.
And no one today knows the happy word "home".
Everyone looks through a strange window.
Some in Tashkent, and some in New York,
and the air of exile is bitter
like poisoned wine.
All of you would have been able to admire me,
when I saved myself from evil pursuit,
in the belly of the flying fish
and flew over the enemy-filled forest
like a witch in the night.

And already, right in front of me,
the Kama was frozen over,
and someone said 'Quo Vadis?'
but his lips did not stir,
and the mad Urals
thundered with bridges and tunnels.
And that road opened out before me
down which so many had gone,
down which they took my son,
and the funeral road was long
among the solemn, crystal
silence of the Siberian land.
From that which had been turned to dust,
seized by death's terror
and knowing the time for vengeance,
with dry eyes lowered,
and wringing its hands,
Russia went to the East,
and I was a witness...

[Finished in Tashkent, 18 August 1942]

314

Anna Akhmatova's Note to *Poem Without a Hero*

...*Triptych* is not connected with any of the works of the 1910s, as the most quadruped readers wish, who in their "simplicity" assume that it is a method of brushing aside the 40s. 'It's old fashioned – that is how people wrote once upon a time.' Who and when? Perhaps it is very bad, but nobody ever wrote like that even in the 1910s.

V.M. Zhirmunsky has written very interestingly about The Poem. He said that it is a fulfilment of the Symbolists' dream. That it is what they preached sermons on in theory, but never realised in their works (the magic of the rhythm, the enchanted vision) and which does not exist in their long poems...For example (Blok about Komissarzhevskaya): B.F. Komissarzhevskaya was singing with a *world* orchestra. That's why her tender yet insistent voice was like the voice of spring – it called us immeasurably further on than the contents of the words that were pronounced.

Zhirmunsky has just this possibility in mind – of calling one immeasurably further on than the words that are pronounced – when he talks about *Poem Without a Hero*. That's why the reader's relationship to The Poem is so varied. Some hear immediately an echo, that second footstep. Others do not hear it.

All this I realised only recently, and it perhaps has become my parting with The Poem.

E.S. Dobin called it the summit of the 20th Century (Komarovo, Summer 1960), X – a requiem for the whole of Europe (1946) [X = Isaiah Berlin. Tr.].

V.V. Cherdyntsev said...

...The struggle with the reader was constant. The reader's help (especially in Tashkent) was too.

So if Berk's words are not just a compliment, *Poem Without a Hero* has the qualities and properties of a completely new work, without precedent in the history of literature, because its reference to music cannot be ascribed to any known work of literature. People started talking about music very early on, back in Tashkent, in connection with *Triptych*. (They pointed to the Schumann (G. Sand) Carnaval), but there the characteristics are given by means of the music itself. The conviction of dance being at its essence (which Pasternak talked about – Russian figures) explains the fact that twice it became a libretto.

Boris Pasternak used to talk about The Poem as a dance. Two Russian figures. 'Retiring with a kerchief' – that is the lyric poetry hiding. 'Advancing, with open hands' – that is The Poem. His words were always unique – there was no repeating or remembering them. They were full of vibrant life.

[Moscow, 14 December 1960]

...In our times the cinema has forced out both tragedy and comedy as pantomime did in Rome. The classical works of Greek drama were turned into pantomime libretti during the Roman Empire. Not a chance analogy perhaps? Is it not the same as Romeo and Juliet (Prokofiev) and Othello being transformed into ballets?

Today M.A. Z[enkevich] was talking at length and in detail about *Triptych*. In his opinion The Poem is a Tragic Symphony: it doesn't need music because it contains it in itself. The author talks as Fate/Anagke soaring above everything – people, times, events. It is solidly constructed. The words are Acmeist, with firmly drawn boundaries. In the fantastical it is close to 'The Tram that Lost its Way' [by N. Gumilyov. Tr.]. In the simplicity of subject matter, which one could express in a couple of words, it is close to *The Bronze Horseman*.

[2 June 1961]

I glimpse the Petersburg period of Russian history from behind the words:
    'Let this place be deserted'
and Suzdal, the Pokrovsk Monastery – Eudoxia Fyodorovna Lopukhina.

The Petersburg terrors: the death of Peter, Paul, Pushkin's duel, the flood, the blockade – all this should be heard in the unrealised music.

The poem is double. A second step is always heard. Something going alongside – another text, and there's no understanding where the voice is or the echo is and which is the shadow of the other, because The Poem is capacious if not bottomless. The lighted torch that has never yet been thrown into it has not yet illuminated it. I penetrate into the tiniest cracks and open them up – that's how the new stanzas appear...Now I realise that the Second Chapter ('Another one is with her') which interferes from the very beginning is made up of omissions, incomplete blanks (There was no Romeo, but there certainly was an Aeneas), out of which almost miraculously, something sometimes can be successfully extracted and put into the text. This is the basis of my reality which so annoys some readers. It upsets me that people call these pieces 'pearls' and they swear that they are better than the surrounding text (this happened with the lyrical interlude about the guest from the future, Chapter One) and the same thing happened recently with the piece 'Somebody is with her "faceless, nameless"...Time to say farewell'...

It's as though I did not so much miss out all the best, surrendering it to, let us say, music, and wrote all the worst, but rather, the best continued to force itself into, and in some places, to burst into the printed text, carrying with it the shadow, the ghost of the music (but never musicality in the bad sense) in which it resided. That is why the "seams" are invisible.

It is impossible to say definitely when I began to hear it. Perhaps it was when I was standing with my companion on Nevsky Prospect (after the dress rehearsal of *The Masquerade*, 25 February 1917) and the cavalry streamed along the pavement like lava or perhaps it was when I was standing (this time without my companion) on the Liteyny bridge at that moment when they opened it in broad daylight to let through the mine carriers to Smolny in support of the Bolsheviks (25 October 1917). How can I tell?

Olga [Glebova-Sudeykina. Tr.] watches a part of my ballet *The Snow Mask* in a box in the theatre. The New Year snowstorm is almost out of Hans Christian Andersen, and visions, perhaps connected with *The Snow Mask* appear in it.

316

This is the apotheosis of the 1910s in all their greatness and weakness. The sense of New Year's Eve and Christmas Eve is the *axis* round which the whole thing revolves, like a magic carousel. It is this breath that stirs all the details and the surrounding air itself. (The wind of tomorrow).

The Poem outgrows its memories and at least once a year (often in December) it demands that I do something with these memories.

> It is the rebellion of things,
> and Koshchei himself
> has sat down on the painted trunk.

I began it in Leningrad (in 1940, my bumper harvest year) and continued it in Tashkent ('*Constantinople pour les pauvres*') which was its magical cradle, then in the last year of the war in Fountain House again among the ruins of my city; and in Moscow and Komarovo among the pines. Alongside it went the mourning *Requiem*, so variegated (although there were no sumptuous epithets) and drowning in the music, whose only accompaniment could be Silence alone and the distant, sparse tolling of the funeral bells. In Tashkent another companion came along – the play *E nu me Elish*, both comic and prophetic, of which not even ashes remain. The lyric poetry did not interfere with it, nor did it interfere with the lyric poetry.

Aided by the music hidden in it, The Poem twice departed from me and became a ballet.

So as I busied myself now with the libretto, now with a film script I still could not grasp what I was doing. The following quotation elucidated the matter: 'This book may be read as a poem or verse play,' Peter Veereck writes (1961 'The Tree Witch') and he explains the techniques by which the poem is transformed into a play. I was doing the same thing at the same time with *Triptych*. Veereck's 'The Tree Witch' is a contemporary of my Poem, and perhaps the closeness...

The Poem's other property is that this magic potion, on flowing into the vessel suddenly thickens and turns into my biography, as though seen by someone in a dream in a series of mirrors. ('And I am happy and sad that I am going with you...') Sometimes I see The Poem as completely transparent, giving off an incomprehensible light (like the light of the white nights, when everything glows from within) unexpected galleries open up, leading no-where, a second step is heard, an echo which considers itself to be the most important and speaks its own words not someone else's; the shadows pretend to be the casters of shadows. Everything doubles and trebles right down to the bottom of the casket.

Suddenly this *Fata Morgana* breaks off. On the table there are just poems, quite elegant, skilful and bold. If there is no mysterious light, no second step, no rebellious echo, no shadows that have received a separate existence, then I begin to understand why it leaves some readers cold. This happens mainly when I read it to someone whom it does not reach, and it comes back to me like a boomerang (forgive the hackneyed simile) and it is distorted and wounds me.

[Komarovo, 17 May 1961]

317

When in June 1941 I read Marina Tsvetayeva part of The Poem (the first draft) she said quite sharply: 'One has to have a lot of nerve to write about Harlequins, Columbines and Pierrots in 1941.' She must have assumed that The Poem is a masterful stylisation in the spirit of Benois and Somov – i.e. that old fashioned claptrap which she was fighting against in the emigration. Time proved otherwise.

The effort to "earth" The Poem (on the advice of the late S.Z. Galkin) ended in complete failure. It categorically refused to 'go into the suburbs'. It didn't want anything to do with the gipsy woman on the spit-strewn pavement, the steam train going to the Virgin in Sorrow, nor Khlebnikov, nor the Hot Field. It did not go with Mayakovsky to death bridge, nor into the 5 kopeck baths, smelling of birch twig brooms, nor to the magical taverns of Blok, with ships on the wall and secrecy and the Petersburg world all around – it stubbornly remained in its fateful corner in the house which was built at the beginning of the 19th century by the Adamini brothers, from which the Marble Palace can be seen, and past which, to the beat of the drum, the snub-nosed recruits from the Pavlov Institute returned to their barracks. The flashes of hundreds of May parades show through the soft, wet New Year snowstorm and

> All the mysteries of the Summer Garden –
> the floods, the meetings, the blockade...

One more interesting point: I have noticed that the more I explain it, the more enigmatic and incomprehensible it becomes. It's clear to everyone that I cannot explain it to its depths, and indeed do not want to (or dare to), and all my explanations (despite their elegance and inventiveness) only complicate the matter – it came from nowhere and has gone off into nowhere, and I have explained nothing...

Only today did I manage to finally formulate my special method (in The Poem). Nothing is said directly. The most complex and deepest things are expressed not in dozens of pages, as people are used to, but in two lines, but two lines that can be understood by everyone.

318

Libretto for Ballet of *Poem Without a Hero*

I. On the darkened stage all that is lit is a table, set for two. Candles. X, with her back to the spectators, with a long black shawl, is sitting, leaning her elbows on the table. The clock shows five to midnight. Conversation with the person who has not come. (He is a portrait, a bust or a *shadow*). A bell rings. Everything changes. A table, the length of the stage – a huge banqueting hall. A crowd of mummers. Everyone is dancing. The demon. Don Juan with Anna in mourning dress. Faust (the old one) with the dead Gretchen. The Milepost (alone). The Goat-footed Nymph leads the Bacchic procession, as if she were on a black-figure vase. X turns away from all of them, and especially herself, at her youngest and with her famous shawl. The 'Guest from the Future' comes out of one of the mirrors, *traverse la scène*, and goes into one of the other mirrors. Everyone is terrified. Columbine's most banal dance. Harlequin and Pierrot. False *bonhomie*. The Cheiromant or Rasputin, (the 'Superfluous Shadow') and everything concerning him. (Limping in his frock coat). He shows everyone their future. Suddenly a man appears, head and shoulders taller than the others, wearing a black cloak and mask. He throws off his cloak, takes off his mask – it is the dragoon boy. The Superfluous Shadow refuses to tell his fortune, but the dragoon insists. In the depth of the stage there is a momentary glimpse of the suicide scene…

Later there should be scenes characterising Petrograd in 1920. (Concluding entry): 'No, not 1920, but 1941 when the bombing first started. Everyone has died long ago.'

II. (The dream of the dragoon: the past and the future). At Columbine's. The *intérieur* of Olga's room. A corner is lit. Portraits of Olga on the walls, which come to life from time to time, and exchange glances, without coming out of the frames. Verka, the little chambermaid, dresses Columbine and puts on her shoes. Mirror. The Superfluous Shadow is reflected in the mirror… Notes and flowers are brought in. The dining room. The dragoon arrives. An intimate breakfast. His jealousy. He takes away a letter and roses. Her promise. Complete agreement. *Pas de deux*. The little hall. She cuts off 'the straw-coloured curl' and gives it to him. (A meeting in the Maltese Chapel). Mozart's Requiem. He chases out the two Harlequins. Reception. The bedroom again. The altar of Venus. But the dragoon is forgotten already. Olga, receives guests, lying in bed in a lace bonnet and nightdress. Candles burn in tall glass candlesticks. 'And the bed is reflected in a round mirror'. And the boy is almost forgotten.

> You are to him, as a magnet to steel.
> Turning pale, he watches through his tears
> how you are handed roses,
> and his enemy is famous.

The guests, Klyuev and Yesenin dance a wild, Russian, sectarian dance. The demon. She inexorably goes to meet him. The first jealousy scene for the dragoon. His despair. An icy chill looks in at the window…The chimes of the clock play a tune. The lame and solicitous one tries to comfort the dragoon, seducing him in a very dark way. 'The Tower' of Vyacheslav

Ivanov – the lame and solicitous one is at home. Antiquity. The altar of Pergamon comes to life. Oedipus and Antigone. A curse. Pagan Russia (Gorodetsky, Stravinsky, The Rite of Spring, Tolstoy, early Khlebnikov) They are outside. The Tavrichesky Garden is covered in snow and the snowstorm is wild. (N.B. even Blok's The Twelve, but unreal and in the distance)...

III. The dragoon by the streetlamp. Meetings: Vera brings a cruel note. Two whores, who have given up on a general, call the dragoon over, but he doesn't go. He thinks he sees her in various guises (as death) at the window with its lace curtains. *(One moment!)* The Noise of Time! The snowstorm. Field of Mars. The Ghosts' Ball. The apparition of a military parade. (Military music). March-past. The lyrical interlude. As in a dream everything interweaves. (Olga watches a part of my ballet *The Snow Mask* in the theatre box.) The dragoon standing by the streetlamp composes poems. Torches. The general again in a military greatcoat. The dragoon is lost in thought and does not notice him. A second curtain rises suddenly in the depth of the stage – there is a terrible staircase, illuminated by a bluish gaslight...Olga returns from the masquerade, with the Stranger. A scene in front of the door. The dragoon is motionless in the *niche*. Their parting leaves nothing to doubt. A kiss. Olga goes into the house. The dragoon's suicide...A shot. The lights dim. Requiem music. Olga comes out and gets down on her knees by the body. The door is left wide open and through it is visible all that will happen and that we know, and beyond it is the unknown Future.

[Krasnaya Konnitsa, 18 December 1959]

Second Variant of the Finale

The door is flung wide open. Columbine comes out in a long black dress, carrying a candle and gets down on her knees by the body. Another figure in a black dress and with a candle mounts the staircase to also stand by the body. Chopin is heard.

[24 December 1959]

*   *   *

(The Superfluous Shadow):
   appears at the ball in the first scene, wearing a white domino costume and a red mask and carrying a spade and a lantern. He has a retinue in the wings that calls him and dances with him. They all scatter. In the second scene he looks in through the window to Columbine's room and is reflected in the mirror, double, treble etc. The mirror shatters into smithereens bringing bad luck.
   In the third scene he gets out of the carriage in an ermine coat and top hat and offers the dragoon a ride. The stars...and the trees in the Mihkailovsky Garden. He (the dragoon) nods his head and shows him the straw-coloured curl. The Superfluous Shadow tries to take the lock with his white-gloved

320

hand. The dragoon takes The Shadow by the hand and the glove is left in his hand for the Shadow never had a hand. He tears the glove in a frenzy.

*   *   *

The Stray Dog – It is Tamara Karsavina's evening – she is dancing in the mirror. Masquerade – a huge fire is burning in the fireplace. Suddenly all the masks become Superfluous Shadows and exchange glances and laugh...

*   *   *

...*Everyone* was at this masquerade. No one sent a refusal. Osip Mandelstam (*'ash on the left shoulder'*), who was already famous but had not yet written a single love poem was there, and Marina Tsvetayeva who had come from Moscow for her 'Otherworldly Evening' and who confused everything in the world...The shadow of Vrubel. All the demons of the XXth Century emerge from him, and there he was himself...The mysterious, village poet Klyuev, and the great Stravinsky who forced the whole of the XXth Century to sound like his music, and the demonic Doctor Dapertutto, and Blok (the tragic tenor of the epoch), deeply depressed for the past five years, and Velimir I (Khlebnikov) as though he had come to the Stray Dog. And Faust – Vyacheslav Ivanov, and Andrey Bely skipping in with his dancer's step and his Manuscript of *Petersburg* under his arm, and the fabulous Tamara Karsavina. I cannot swear that Rozanov's glasses do not gleam there in the corner, and is not that Rasputin's flowing beard, in the depth of the hall, the stage, or hell (I don't know which)? At times there is the sound of thunder, or is it Chaliapin's voice? And there the Tsarskoye Selo swan, or is it Anna Pavlova, floats past, and Mayakovsky, before he met Brik, is smoking a cigarette by the fire...(but in the depths of the 'dead' mirrors, which come to life and start to gleam with a suspiciously murky sparkle, and in their depths the one-legged, old organ-grinder (for thus is Fate attired) shows to all those gathered there – their future, and their end.). Nijinsky's last dance, Meyerhold's departure. The only person who is missing is the one who definitely ought to be there, and not only be there, but be standing on the landing and meeting the guests...Moreover:

> We should drink to him
> who is not with us yet.

[6–7 January 1962]

Translator's Notes to the Poems

WHITE FLOCK   (67–80)

75. **Dream:** '...the Tsaritsa's Garden': this poem is probably set in the park in
Tsarskoye Selo (the Royal Village), outside St Petersburg (now Pushkin, outside
Leningrad), which is a recurring motif in Akhmatova's work.

75. **'I still see hilly Pavlovsk':** Pavlovsk, like Tsarskoye Selo, is outside Leningrad
and has a palace (built 1782–6) and a fine park with statuary, such as Apollo, the
lyre-bearer (Citharode). This poem is one of several dedicated to N.V. Nedobro-
vo, Akhmatova's friend who also wrote an article on her earliest poetry that she
judged in later life as the finest piece of criticism on her poetry, anticipating many
later themes. Her relationship with him and his attitude to her writing have
prompted one Russian critic to say that 'Nedobrovo made Akhmatova'. He died
of TB in 1919.

WAYSIDE GRASS   (81–96)

95. **'I asked the cuckoo':** Tradition has it in Russian folklore that the number of
times the cuckoo cries in answer to this question is the number of years the
questioner will live. Cf. the silence of the cuckoo in *Poem Without a Hero*.

ANNO DOMINI   (97–112)

98. **Lullaby:** Nikolai Gumilyov, Akhmatova's husband and father of Lev, was
twice awarded the George Cross for bravery while serving as a volunteer in
France in the First World War.

98. **Little Song:** In the Russian the poem is an acrostic to Boris Anrep,
Akhmatova's friend, the artist, mosaicist and poet. He went to England in 1916
and stayed in the West, meeting Akhmatova 50 years later in Paris. His mosaic of
Anna Akhmatova is in the National Gallery in London. A whole mythology
arose about the black ring which Akhmatova's Tatar grandmother had given her
which she gave to Anrep on his departure to England. The ring is mentioned
several times in Akhmatova poems not in this collection and also in 'Black Songs'
(p.219). Gleb Struve has written an essay, which includes a Memoir by Anrep in
Volume III of the Works of Akhmatova. Anrep, who had 'beckoned' Akhmatova
to the West, shortly after his emigration, to his considerable embarrassment, lost
the 'magical' ring.

101. **'Terror rummaging through things in the dark':** Nikolai Gumilyov, was
shot, aged 36, on or around 24 August 1921, for not revealing his knowledge of
an anti-Bolshevik plot. He has recently been published for the first time in 60
years. In 1988 two separate large books of his poetry were published in Tiflis and
Leningrad. Akhmatova reacted sharply to some of the "biographical" material in
the four-volume Western Collection of Nikolai Gumilyov (Washington, 1961)
edited by Struve and Filippov, but his poetry and memory were dear to her. Their
only son, Lev, born in 1912, who was mainly looked after by his grandmother on
the Gumilyov Estate in Slepnyovo, was to suffer – right up to the labour camps –
apparently because of his parents.

101. Slander: Years later Stalin is said to have taken vigorous exception to this poem.

102. Black Dreams: Cycle written to Akhmatova's second husband, Shileyko.

105. The Third Zachatevsky Sidestreet where Akhmatova lived with Shileyko in Moscow for a year in 1918.

107. Biblical Poems: In her later years Akhmatova intended, according to Joseph Brodsky (*Kontinent* 53), to put many Bible stories into verse.

111. New Year Ballad, with its premonition in the last lines of the 'guest from the future' and the wine burning like poison became central to *Poem Without a Hero*.

REED *(113–36)*

114. Inscription in a Book: Mikhail Lozinsky, fellow poet, member of the Guild of Poets, friend and magazine editor, sympathetic to Acmeism, translator of Dante and Shakespeare. Akhmatova completed her memoir of him shortly before her death in 1966.

115. 'One can leave this life so simply': Written on Yesenin's suicide.

116. 'Here Pushkin's exile began': The last line in the original is: 'the immortal lover of Tamara' from Lermontov's poem 'The Demon'.

121. Boris Pasternak: In 1928 Boris Pasternak had written a poem 'To Anna Akhmatova'. After Pasternakian fireworks of country and town, the last two verses read:

> This is how I see your image and appearance.
> It is not inspired by that pillar of salt,
> with which five years ago you nailed
> the terror of the backward look into poetry.

> But emerging from your first books
> where the seeds of intense prose were growing
> in everything, like sparks on a lightning conductor
> it forces events to strike reality.

This poem indicates the recurrent Orpheus/Eurydice/Lot's wife theme in Akhmatova, as well as reinforcing Mandelstam's comments on Akhmatova's prose origins. The poem's detail caused Chukovskaya to maintain to Akhmatova that her friend and supporter Pasternak had indeed read at least her earlier poetry.

122. Voronezh: Akhmatova visited the Mandelstams in exile in Voronezh in 1936. Emma Gerstein in 'Novoe o Mandelstame' ('New Material on Mandelstam') makes a case that the last four lines of 'Voronezh' were written after Mandelstam's death in 1938.

The *verdigris* dome is one of the only words which I have borrowed from any of the English translations, which I read at a very late stage in the making of this book, abiding by Lozinsky's advice to Akhmatova not to read her translator 'forerunners' early on. In this case the "loan word" is from the excellent small bilingual book *Poems of Akhmatova*, translated by Stanley Kunitz with Max Hayward (Collins Harvill, 1974). Other translations I consulted: *You Will Hear Thunder*, translated by D.M. Thomas (Secker and Warburg, 1985), reissued as *Anna Akhmatova: Selected Poems* (Penguin Books, 1988); *Anna Akhmatova:*

Selected Poems, translated by Walter Arndt, Robin Kemball and Carl Proffer (Ardis, 1976); and *Anna Akhmatova: Poems*, translated by Lyn Coffin (Norton, 1983). We all share a love of Akhmatova.

123. **Dante:** Akhmatova turns us with her quotation from Dante's *Inferno*, Canto XIX.17, to the 'baptisings in my beautiful San Giovanni', in Florence, which turns the reader to the opening of Canto XXV of *Paradiso*, in the Singleton translation: 'If ever it come to pass that the sacred poem to which heaven and earth have so set hand that it has made me lean for many years should overcome the cruelty which bars me from the fair sheepfold where I slept as a lamb, an enemy to the wolves which war on it, with changed voice now and with changed fleece a poet will I return, and *at the font of my baptism* will I take the crown.' This poem, central to Akhmatova's concept of the poet and the State, possibly concerns Osip Mandelstam, Akhmatova's co-reader of Dante, who was in exile in Voronezh with his wife Nadezhda at the time of the writing of this poem. Akhmatova uses a novel treatment of the Orpheus and Eurydice theme – where the poet does *not* look round.

123. **A Little Geography:** Leningrad becomes the transit station for a mass forced exodus to the labour camps in Siberia and Central Asia. 'All change for Freedom Camp' is Ronald Hingley's title for a chapter of *Nightingale Fever* (Weidenfeld and Nicholson) an enthralling account of Akhmatova, Mandelstam, Pasternak and Tsvetayeva. 'A Little Geography' is discussed by Nadezhda Mandelstam in *Hope Against Hope* (Penguin edition, p.381).
Irgiz is in the north of Akyubinskaya in Soviet Central Asia. Ishim is north west of Omsk and Atbasar is on the railway near Akmolinsk in Soviet Central Asia.

124. **Fragments of Pottery:** 'You cannot leave your mother an orphan': this inexact Joyce quotation, identified by James Christie and Martin Novelli, is from *Ulysses* (Penguin edition, p.412; Bodley Head edition, p.543):

> You have spoken of the past and its phantoms, Stephen said...All desire to see you bring forth the work you meditate. I heartily wish you may not fail them. O no, Vincent, Lenehan said...have no fear. He could not leave his mother an orphan.

Both Akhmatova (in the original) and Mandelstam in a 'good Russian translation' read Joyce in the 30s. Akhmatova considered this epigraph to be of vital importance and told her English friend, Peter Norman, that it should be applied to the whole of *Requiem*. In the 1987 Soviet edition of her work it is applied (again misquoted in the Notes) to the poem 'Crucifixion', part X of *Requiem*, most of which is left out of that edition. 'Fragments of Pottery', with a commentary by Lydia Chukovskaya, has recently been published in the magazine *Gorizont*. Chukovskaya had also suggested to Akhmatova that the lines 'I stand, on the shameful scaffold of disaster / as if I were under the canopy of a throne' could be an epigraph for her poetry.
Chouane: a Royalist rebel during the French Revolution.
Emma Gerstein, in an article published in *Russian Literary Triquarterly*, goes in detail into the fate of Akhmatova's son Lev Gumilyov, now a retired professor of Turkic languages and culture. He first came across these languages in labour camps in Central Asia. He had a difficult relationship with his mother, hinted at already in 'Lullaby' (p.98), from 1915. Nadezhda Mandelstam has mentioned his 'hostage' status for Akhmatova's poems of the 30s, 40s and 50s.

125. **Imitation of the Armenian:** written after one of the arrests of her son Lev, in

the mid or late 30s. It would have been obvious to whom this desperately dangerous poem was written had it been circulated. It remains a monument to what Akhmatova called the 'non-vegetarian' times.

126. Between the Cathedral of the Spilt Blood on the site where Alexander II was assassinated in 1881, and the Engineer (Mikhailovsky) Castle where his grandfather Paul I was murdered in 1801. Field of Mars: cf. *Poem Without a Hero.*

126. Gogol's Viy had long eyelashes. Equally Viy is a monster in Ukrainian folklore, mentioned one of Mandelstam's last poems. Morozova, the noblewoman, was an Old Believer, persecuted for her beliefs. A famous picture by the artist Surikov depicts her going off into exile.

127. **The Cellar of Memory:** Akhmatova has in mind Khlebnikov's long poem in vol. IV (p.231) of the Slavische Propylaea Edition, *Forest Horror:* 'O, cellar of memory! I've not been/ down there for a long time!/...Are you ready to come down with me/ into the cellar of the soul?/ Anyone who wants to go grey early/ should sit there all night.' From further evidence in Khlebnikov's poem it is obvious that the cellar is that of the Stray Dog Café/Cabaret, which had its day in 1912–15. Akhmatova regarded Khlebnikov as crazy, but brilliant; without the condescension that usually implies.

129. The Pushkin epigraph is from an extra part of a poem (formerly entitled 'Cleopatra') introduced into 'Egyptian Nights'. Whereas Pushkin's poem concerns earlier feasting incidents, Akhmatova's Cleopatra is at the end of her life as described by Shakespeare. The epigraph from *Antony and Cleopatra* (V. 2. 289), 'I am fire and air (the other elements I give to baser life)', was a favourite one of Akhmatova's.

129. **Stanzas:** This poem about the Kremlin, past and and at the time of writing, introduces the theme of the Streltsy, the soldiers tortured and executed under Peter the Great. Their womenfolk pleaded for them under the Kremlin walls. The analogy with the situation of Akhmatova and hundreds of thousands of her contemporaries would be obvious, hence this, as *Requiem* in which the Streltsy women are also mentioned, was one of the poems that were not published in her lifetime.

131. **'So the dark souls fly off':** *Enkidu:* The companion of Gilgamesh. In the Russian, Akhmatova uses the earlier transcription Aebani. She was familiar with the Epic of Gilgamesh from the collaborative translation (1921) by Nikolai Gumilyov, Lozinsky and her second husband, the Assyriologist Shileyko.

133. **'So in defiance':** As often in Akhmatova epigraphs, she slightly distorts the quotation – in this case combining two lines from an early version of a Zabolotsky poem, obscure enough to fox even Chukovskaya for some time.

134. **Splitting Up:** Akhmatova later said she should have split up with Punin many years earlier. Their period together did indeed coincide with her least productive period of writing poems. She told Chukovskaya that she did not write any poems for 13 years (this period ending in 1936).

135. **Inscription in the Book *Wayside Grass*:** 'The mysterious artist' is the artist/illustrator (also of Akhmatova's early books) M.V. Dobuzhinsky (1875–1957).

136. **'Leningrad in March 1941':** The Menshikov Palace is on the Neva embankment on Vasiliev Island.

SEVENTH BOOK (137–204)

Secrets of the Craft: Originally included the second part of the poem to Osip Mandelstam, which is in *A Wreath for the Dead* in this collection.
8. *On Poetry:* Vladimir Narbut (1888–1938), poet on the naturalist wing of the Acmeist movement, whom Gumilyov and N. Kharzhiev (Moscow critic and friend of Akhmatova) rated highly.

146. **In 1940:** Akhmatova turns to war-torn Europe and 'the burial of the epoch'.

2. *To the Londoners:* Shakespeare's 24th play, the one that Shakespeare did not write: more tragic and historical than any other. There is also an element of Pushkin's 'Feast in the Time of the Plague', from the English of John Wilson. *To the Londoners* in one version has an epigraph from the Apocalypse: 'Battle is joined in the sky.'
3. *Shadow:* The epigraph is from drafts of a Mandelstam poem 'Straw Girl' (straw is *soloma* in Russian) of 1916 to Salomeya Andronikova (Halpern). There is a line in the poem: 'all twelve months sing about the hour of death'. She was one of the 'beauties of 1913' or Mandelstam's 'tender Europeans', and was a friend of Akhmatova's in Petersburg. After the revolution she emigrated, and lived in London until her death in 1982.
4. *'Didn't I know sleeplessness':* In all Russian printed texts Normandy is printed instead of Finland, which Akhmatova could not write at the time. Russia went to war with Finland in 1939 before joining the Second World War, taking much of its land, including the area round Komarovo, where Akhmatova was to live her last years. Komarovo (Finnish name Raivola) is 40km from Leningrad on the Vyborg road. Finland's great Modernist poet Edith Södergran (1892–1923) lived in Raivola for most of her life, and Anna Akhmatova is buried there. Other references to Finland are in 'Happy New Year' (p.127) and the real draft of 10 of *The Sweetbriar in Bloom* (p.195), and 'The North' (p.233).

149-54. **Wind of War:** A cycle of war poems (two of which I have not included). 'Courage' was published in *Pravda* on 8 March 1942. With the war Akhmatova seemed to be going to have the opportunity to publish again, and write more freely.

154-66: Poems written near Tashkent where Akhmatova was evacuated from November 1941 to May 1943.

176. **Death:** Akhmatova was seriously ill with typhus and went to the sanatorium in Dyurmen, near Tashkent. II. The line 'There is a cabin for me on this ship' is from a single line fragment of Osip Mandelstam from 1937. Perhaps this poem should be connected with Akhmatova's final quatrain in *A Half Century of Quatrains* (p.246) about the ship 'Queen Death'.

157-62. **The Moon in the Zenith:** Madame Fifi, in Maupassant's story of the same name, was the nickname of a German officer, distinguished for his exceptional cruelty. Lutfi was the 15th century Uzbek lyric poet, on whose poetry Akhmatova worked with others as a translator. 10. *The Moon Comes Out* is dedicated to Alexey Kozlovsky who composed music to *Poem Without a Hero*. He and his wife were close friends of Akhmatova in Tashkent. Heser was the hero of the Central Asian epic the Heseriad.

163. **'It was your lynx eyes, Asia':** Termez is in Central Asia near the Soviet/ Afghan border.

166. **'I would not have seen the quince flower bloom'**: Aybek is the name of the Uzbek writer Musa Tashmukhamedov (1905–68).

167. **The Plane:** Lydia Chukovskaya, on questioning Akhmatova about the wording of II, elicited from her this original variant concerning Garshin's abandonment of her, which changes the whole tone of the poem:

> It would have been better for me to have beaten
> his damned body up to the neck into the ground,
> if I had known what I was flying to meet
> as the plane outstripped the sun.
> [Leningrad, June 1944]

Akhmatova considered that the siege of Leningrad had disturbed the balance of Dr Vladimir Garshin's mind. He was the nephew of the famous short story writer Vsevolod Garshin. Lydia Chukovskaya says he is the addressee of the poem 'The man who means nothing to me now' (p.180).

173. **Youth:** The 'young hand' or actually 'hands' in the Russian was originally 'fifteen year old hands', setting the poem in 1905. The Shukhardin House in Tsarskoye Selo, where Akhmatova lived from early childhood to the age of sixteen (and where she met the Gumilyov brothers), was knocked down in 1905. Akhmatova considered herself virtually homeless or houseless for most of her life, although she had friends who made her welcome, especially in Moscow. Concerts were held at the Pavlovsk Station (see Mandelstam's 1921 poem 'Concert at the Station'). The Babolov Palace was constructed in 1783 in the Babolov Park in Tsarskoye Selo.

175. **Hearthwarming:** 1. *Mistress of the House:* Yelena Bulgakov, the wife of Mikhail Bulgakov, novelist and author of *Master and Margarita*, lived in the same house as Akhmatova. Both Nadezhda Mandelstam (who was also in Tashkent at this time) and Yelena Bulgakov were to be vigorous defenders and preservers of their dead husbands' writings.

177. **Near Kolomna:** Akhmatova stayed with the Shervinskys at their dacha in Starki outside Moscow in 1936, 1952 and 1956. Sergey Shervinsky was a translator. Akhmatova wrote parts of *The Sweetbriar in Bloom* there, and has mentioned that the flower itself really did bloom wildly.

178. **'All the souls...'** dated in some cases 1944, but could be as early as 1921.

181. **'It is no wonder that my unruly poems'**: Between the two verses in this poem, where the Phlegethon is the fiery river that circles Hades, there were at one time eight further lines:

> Those with whom I drank wine in the cellar,
> my elegant rivals and enemies,
> and those who read me their poems:
> their voices and footsteps have fallen silent,
> and those with whom I shared bad bread,
> with whom I carried on conversations in the black years,
> and those with whom I waited to return to my native city
> under the stars in the Asian sky...

188. **Second Anniversary:** of Akhmatova's return to Leningrad on 31 May 1944.

189. Cinque: These poems were written shortly after Isaiah Berlin's visit to Akhmatova in autumn 1945. She presented the second to him before he left for Moscow. The choice of the Baudelaire epigraph from the poem 'Une Martyre' (A Martyred Woman) from *Fleurs du mal* CX is apposite enough at the end of that poem. In the Francis Scarfe translation, *Baudelaire: The Complete Verse* (Anvil Press, 1986), the last verse reads: 'Now your partner roams the earth, and your immortal shade keeps watch over him wherever he may sleep; and no doubt as steadfastly as you, he will be faithful and constant to the death.' The headless corpse of the woman in the picture that Baudelaire vividly describes in the earlier part of his poem may not seem relevant, until we find Akhmatova referring to Keats' *Isabella; or, the Pot of Basil* in *The Sweetbriar in Bloom* and *Madame de Lamballe* in *Poem Without a Hero*, both of whom are involved with headlessness. I believe this is psychologically important to the poetry, but do not hasten to draw any conclusions.

191-97. The Sweetbriar in Bloom: Written about her meetings, and non-meetings with Isaiah Berlin, who visited Russia in 1945, and with his wife in 1956, on which occasion he did not see Akhmatova; but this non-meeting ten years after their first was important to Akhmatova who, fearful for her son's safety after the consequences of their first meeting, only spoke to Berlin on the phone. Their final meeting in Oxford was 20 years after their first. The epigraph from Keats, one of Akhmatova's favourite poets, is from *Isabella; or, the Pot of Basil* (XXXIX).
7. Dmitry Donskoy led his army from Moscow against the Tatars down the road in 1380.
11. Akhmatova strongly identified herself with Dido, see also 'The Last Rose'. Here she takes Aeneas' self-justificatory words from Virgil's *Aeneid* as an epigraph.
12. There was an epigraph from Dante's *Purgatorio* (XXX. 46). In Charles S. Singleton's translation: 'Not a drop of blood is left in me that does not tremble: I know the tokens of the ancient flame.' This is the section when Dante meets Beatrice.
14. Jerusalem was destroyed during the rule of Emperor Vespasian 69−79 AD.

199-204. Midnight Verses: These poems are again connected with Isaiah Berlin.
3. The epigraph is from Horace's *Odes* (3. 26), addressed to Venus, goddess of love. Lewis Carroll's *Alice through the Looking Glass* was translated into Russian in 1924. The epigraph is from the French poet Gérard de Nerval's 'El Deschidado'.

206. Music: Shostakovich was evacuated from Leningrad to Moscow in 1942. Akhmatova had a special relationship to Shostakovich's music, especially his Seventh (Leningrad) Symphony, numerologically connected with her *Seventh Book*, and *Seventh* (incomplete) *Elegy*. The Seventh Symphony is mentioned in an early variant of the ending of *Poem Without a Hero*. She bore out of besieged Leningrad the first part of the Symphony on her lap in the plane in 1941.

207. Summer Garden: the main park in Leningrad, by the Neva embankment. In 1924 it was flooded by the Neva.

208. 'Don't frighten me': V. Zhirmunsky, who died before his (censored) Biblioteka Poeta Edition of Anna Akhmatova came out in 1973, told Isaiah Berlin that Akhmatova wrote this poem for him.

209. To Pushkin's Town: The origin of the name Tsarskoye Selo (Royal Village – which indeed it was in imperial times) is from the Finnish word *sarsk*, which means "island". Akhmatova retains this spelling, as Pushkin did on occasion, in 'Heiress' (p.184).

210. Little Songs: *Love Song* is (according to V. Zhirmunsky) for Isaiah Berlin.

212. *From* The Cycle of Tashkent Pages: This poem is for Josef Czapski – the first foreigner she had met since the First World War, a Polish officer, who had joined up with the expeditionary force shortly after he had been released from two years labour camp in Soviet Central Asia. A cultured man, and an artist, he subsequently wrote books on his experiences in the Soviet Union and worked in the Polish émigré press in Paris.

214. 'Distance collapsed in rubble': Almost an ecological poem, from the end of the 50s, on the concept of man's accelerating change. The Soviet experiments to reverse the rivers and disastrous agricultural policies may be indicated here.

215. 'These praises do not become me': The Oxford orator's reference to Sappho at the honorary degree giving ceremony must have rung strangely in Akhmatova's ears.

217. Three Verses: Zhukovsky street was where Akhmatova lived in Tashkent. The Rogachev Highway led from Moscow to Alexander Blok's estate at Shakhmatovo.
III. cf. Alexander Blok's poem of 10 October 1912:

> Night, a streetlamp, a chemist's,
> a senseless and dull light.
> A quarter of a century will pass –
> you'll still find everything like this. No outcome.

> When you die everything will begin again
> and repeat itself as before: night,
> the icy ripple of the canal,
> the chemist's, and the streetlamp.

219. Black Songs: Boris Anrep, to whom these songs are dedicated, wanted Akhmatova to follow him into emigration.

221. A Page of Ancient History, *Alexander at Thebes*: 'the house of the Poet' is that of the Greek Pindar (518–442 BC) left untouched on Alexander's orders in the destruction of Thebes in 335 BC.

222. Petersburg in 1913: A poem from the fragments surrounding the *Poem Without a Hero*. The 'Hot Field', quite by chance is a literal and adequate translation for the area on the outskirts of Petersburg where thieves and the underworld gathered.

223. Tsarskoye Selo Ode: The *Cypress Chest* is the title of Annensky's book (published posthumously) which made such a deep impression on Akhmatova. Temnik(ov) is in Mordovia, Shuya is north-east of Vladimir. Their significance to the poem seems to me to be in their remoteness. Vitebsk was Chagall's home town, which he painted in his early work.
'Tsar's vodka': I reinsert these words into the original, and leave the variant 'until late' which remains in the Russian text. Joseph Brodsky, in a discussion with Solomon Volkov in *Kontinent* 53, describes how Naiman revealed that 'Tsar's

vodka' in Russian smacked of an acid or chemical formula, and so she rejected it. I felt it was important to put it back in the translation.

225. **Our Own Land:** The Russian 'melim, mesim i kroshim' translates directly as 'mill, mess and crush'.

225. **The Last Rose:** See note to 126.

232. **Twenty-three Years Later:** Also tied in with *Poem Without a Hero,* which begins with the lighting of the sacred candles.

233. **In Memory of V.S. Sreznevskaya:** Akhmatova's lifelong friend, at the end of her life, helped her with some of her autobiographical prose, which Akhmatova corrected but left in the third person.

234. **Imitation of the Korean:** Akhmatova translated from literal translations (the famous, detailed *podstrochniki*) from 30 different languages – including Korean and Armenian of which she did Imitations. Apart from Leopardi (with Naiman) and Tagore, and ancient Egyptian poetry, she did not take on very major poets (she turned down offers to translate French poets whom she knew well), but was a working translator, apparently squeezing her own poems in between for long periods at a time. This was partly due to financial pressures. Her translations were widely published.

A HALF CENTURY OF QUATRAINS *(239–246)*

I made up this title to gather together these 50 odd quatrains from Akhmatova's fifty years of writing. These poems bring out a different, more colloquial Akhmatova. Their creative bitingness and bitterness affected me deeply.
Wolf Field: In Russian the cemetery outside Leningrad Volkovo Field: I use Wolf as a proper name originating from Volk.

EPIC AND DRAMATIC FRAGMENTS *(247–86)*

Epic Motifs: 2. The artist is Nathan Isaevich Altman (1889–1970) who in 1944 was painting the famous portrait of Akhmatova in blue (with Cubist angles) which is in the Russian Museum in Leningrad. It appears on the cover of *Anna of All the Russias* by Jessie Davies (Collets, 1988).

Northern Elegies: Akhmatova wrote a quatrain:

There will be four: this is what I decided,
and now it's time to test fate.
The first has already completed
its journey to the column of shame.

A couple of lines of the Seventh Elegy (which Akhmatova indicates was very important to her) were published by Lydia Chukovskaya in the magazine *Gorizont* in 1987. The fact that the full text of *Fragments of Pottery* is published by Chukovskaya with this article, and that *Requiem* has also been published in the Soviet Union, would seem to indicate that we are nearing complete publication of Akhmatova's work.
The Elegies are monologues, written in vers libre. *The First:* on this occasion alone I have taken the responsibility for putting what would normally be, either a given for the Russian reader, or a scholarly note into the text of this poem: the Karamazov's village for Staraya Russa, Father Seraphim – the model for

Dostoyevsky's Father Zosima at Optina, Akhmatova's mother's name Inna, and Dostoyevsky, the Omsk convict.

The Third: 'Fifteen years': the time spent with her second husband N. Punin in Fountain House, until they split up in 1938.

The Seventh: the basis of the Seventh Elegy seems to be that of 'the last speech of the accused' (according to Chukovskaya). We have three lines that do little to vocalise the silence:

> And I am silent. I've been silent for thirty years.
> Silence like Arctic icebergs...
>
> And I am silent...As though my brother has died.

Prologue: *Fragments of a Tragedy or a Dream within a Dream:* There is confusion about the real nature of this Play, which Akhmatova burnt in the 40s, for reasons of safety (cf. 'Cinque', 4). Nadezhda Mandelstam in *Hope Abandoned* (Penguin edition, p. 396) describes the version she saw shortly after Akhmatova wrote it in Tashkent. It was in three parts, the first and third in prose. The second part, *Dream within a Dream,* Akhmatova rewrote in the 60s, and is in verse. The third part (and the most controversial, dealing with a writer's trial) seems to be connected with what is known of the Seventh Elegy, thus giving credence that this was a very important poem. The play *E nu ma Elish* ('From Above'), taken from an ancient Assyrian play translated by her second husband Shileyko, seems to be a blind alley in connection with Akhmatova's play, but given Akhmatova's attachment to the title there would seem to be some definite connection. Olophern was Nebuchanezzar's general. He was murdered by Judith.

The Big Confession has only been published recently, and seems to be interconnected with *Prologue.*

4. Francesca: In Dante's *Inferno* (V. 133–8) Francesca da Rimini tells Dante how she and Paolo were reading about Lancelot: 'A Gallehault was the book and he who wrote it; that day we read no farther in it.' Gallehault urged Queen Guinevere to first kiss Lancelot, and so was a "go-between".

LONG POEMS *(267–286)*

By the Sea Shore: This poem was written in 1914 and published in 1915 in the magazine *Apollon* and subsequently in book form in 1921. Akhmatova had been impressed by Blok's *Italian Poems* in *Russkaya Mysl* of 1914. He wrote to her in 1916, congratulating her and saying that after reading it he 'felt again that he loved poetry'. The poem, set in the Crimea, is seen through the eyes of a 14 year old girl (with a disabled twin sister). Akhmatova wrote that 'this meant that I said goodbye to my young days in the Chersonese and the "wild girl" and sensed the iron advance of war'.

From 1896 to 1903 Akhmatova spent every summer on the shores of the Streletskaya Bay, which is a few miles west of Sebastopol. The Chersonese is the south-westernmost point of the Crimea. Balaklava and Inkerman ('French bullets' and 'rusted splinters of heavy shells') are both in this area. Cape Fiolent lies across the steppe a few miles south-east of the Chersonese on which stands the ruined Greek city of Korsun (Old Russian name for the Greek Cherson). Constantine's battery commanded the entrance to the main harbour of Sebastopol. The lighthouse referred to was probably Inkerman, east of the Chersonese. Outside Sebastopol, near Streletskaya Bay, was the church of St Vladimir. The monastery of St George was on the cliffs of Cape Fiolent.

The Way of All the Earth: The epigraph is a combination of the Biblical, from II Kings (2. 2): 'Now the days of David drew night that he should die; and he charged Solomon his son, saying: *'I go the way of all the earth:* be thou strong therefore, and shew thyself a man'; and similarly from Vladimir Monomakh's homily to his children as he gets on his sledge for his final ride.

Kitezh is a city that in fable was saved from the Tatars by disappearing into a lake. Bells ringing could sometimes be heard (? The Kitezh woman heard the wrong chimes).

The poem moves back in time, from the outbreak of World War II (1), to the trenches of World War I, and the tattered map of Europe, and her last visit to the Crimea in 1916 (2), to her childhood (5) and the Tsushima disaster, that she, as a daughter of a naval father felt particularly keenly. The *Koreyets* and the *Varyag*, after making their way from the north of Russia, via the English Channel, were sunk by the Japanese at Tsushima. The heroism and futility were in equal parts. *Fort Shabrol* was the name for the house on Shabrol Street in Paris where the anti-Dreyfus conspirators held out in 1899. In 6, 'calmly sitting on the light sledge' amounts in Russian symbolism to accepting death – tying the poem in with the two epigraphs at the beginning.

Requiem: *Foreword:* 'The Yezhov Terror', known in Russia as Yezhovshchina. Yezhov was head of Stalin's secret police during the Great Terror, and was himself purged. *Requiem* is one of those very rare poems that is both a good poem and a good historical document. Its publication in the Soviet Union (1987) means that it has now been officially handed over to the peoples of the Soviet Union. *Introduction:* 'Russia': 'Rus' in the Russian, the traditional name for Russia. **I:** This poem describes the first arrest of Akhmatova's second husband Nikolai Punin, art historian and scholar. Akhmatova did herself go to officials in the Kremlin and on this occasion he was released very quickly. He subsequently died in labour camp.

'Like the Streltsy wives': see note to page 129.

IV: *The Crosses Prison* – 'Kresty': a prison built of the Vyborg side of St Petersburg in 1893. It literally means 'Crosses' (referring to the layout of the buildings) and the additional sense of 'standing before the cross' should be borne in mind. Cf. parts 6 & 10. Nikolai Gumilyov (in 1921), Nikolai Punin (Akhmatova's husbands) and her son Lev Gumilyov were all in the Crosses Prison at different times.

VII: *Sentence:* the poem is dated the day of Lev Gumilyov's sentence to labour camp.

VIII: *To Death:* 'the blue cap' of the NKVD man; the 'janitor' had to be present at an arrest.

'poison'd shot of slander': Anatoly Naiman points to Claudius' speech in Shakespeare's *Hamlet* (IV 1): '...slander...as the cannon to his blank/ Transports his *poison'd shot'*.

The Yenisey river in Siberia was where many of the concentration/labour camps were.

X: *Crucifixion:* The epigraph 'Weep not for me Mother,/ when thou lookest in the grave' is from the Russian Orthodox Matins for Easter Saturday. See page 124. Peter Norman's recording of *Requiem* shows that the second line of the above epigraph is 'vo grobe zryashe', not – as printed in Struve/Filippov – 'vo grobe sushchu' (I am in the grave).

Requiem has at last (1987) been published in the Soviet Union in the magazines

Neva and *Oktyabr*, almost fifty years after it was composed: not written, for only a handful of honoured, trustworthy people learned it by heart (among them Nadezhda Mandelstam and Lydia Chukovskaya).

POEM WITHOUT A HERO *(287–314)*

The epigraph 'Some are no more, others are far away' is from the 13th century Persian poet Saadi's *Bostan* via Pushkin's *Eugene Onegin* (VIII. 51): 'Those to whom I read/ these lines at meetings of friends,/ some are no more, others are far away/ as Saadi once said.' It was earlier used by Pushkin as an epigraph to 'Bakhchisarai Fountain' referring to his Decembrist friends, hanged or sent to Siberia. It incorporates the contemporary Russian 'Toast no.2': 'To absent friends.'

First Dedication: 27 December 1940. The date is the second anniversary of Osip Mandelstam's date of death. At one stage (and in reprintings) the First Dedication bore the initials of Vesvolod Knyazev, the cornet of Dragoons. Nadezhda Mandelstam discusses this doubling up of disparate characters (the minor poet who committed suicide and the major poet who lived out his fate) in *Hope Abandoned* (Penguin edition, pp.488–90). Knyazev's book of poems was published in a small edition in 1914, after his suicide.

Second Dedication; To Olga Glebova-Sudeikina, actress friend of Akhmatova's, one of the 'beauties of 1913'. She played the role of Confuser Psyche on stage and the 'goat-legged nymph', frequented the Stray Dog Cabaret, which her artist husband had decorated with murals. She emigrated to France and died on 20 January 1945.

Third Dedication: To the Guest from the Future. For Isaiah Berlin, the Oxford philosopher, who visited Akhmatova by chance in November 1945. This Dedication was added after Berlin's visit to the Sheremetev Palace (Fountain House). The grandiose names conceal the fact that Fountain House was divided into sparsely furnished flats, reached by a dark staircase.
Once on an Epiphany Evening. Zhukovsky: The opening lines of Vasily Zhukovsky's ballad *Svetlana* (1808–12).
The Bach Chaconne, solo piece for violin from Bach's Partita no.2 in D minor.

Chapter One: The first epigraph is from Da Ponte's libretto to Mozart's *Don Giovanni*: 'You will stop laughing before the dawn'. The second epigraph is from Akhmatova's poem of January 1914: 'I used to like to warm myself by the fire/ after the wind and the frost. The third epigraph is from *Eugene Onegin* (V.10). Tatiana, like Svetlana in the Zhukovsky ballad, wants to tell her fortune and conjure up her lover. She gets frightened and Pushkin says 'let's not tell fortunes with Tatiana'.
'In my hot youth when George the Third was king' is from Byron's *Don Juan* (I. 212); 'the wine burns like poison' is from Akhmatova's poem 'New Year Ballad' (p.111) prefiguring the Guest from the Future theme.
Dapertutto: pseudonym for Vsevolod Meyerhold, the theatre director, taken from a Hoffman story. Glahn: hero of Hamsun's novel *Pan*. Dorian: from Oscar Wilde's *Picture of Dorian Gray*. Hamlet's garters from *Hamlet* II.1.
Man in the Iron Mask: the prisoner of the Bastille. Lord of Darkness: Mephistopheles, who appears in Goethe's *Faust*. The artist at mocking: seems to be the

poet Kuzmin. For all these characters see also Akhmatova's Libretto for Ballet of *Poem Without a Hero*.

The 'guest from the future' and the poet are the only 'living' people among the ghosts.

Cagliostro: Giuseppe Balzamo, a charlatan who flourished round the time of the French Revolution. Lysisca was the pseudonym of the Empress Messalina.

Mamre Oak: cf. Genesis. Hammurabi: King of Babylon 1792–1750 BC. Lycurgus and Solon: ancient Greek half-mythical law-givers from Sparta and Athens respectively.

'I am ready for death': the exact words of Osip Mandelstam to Akhmatova, fusing the the characters of Mandelstam and Knyazev. 'Between the stove and the cupboard' has been taken to be an allusion to Kirillov's suicide in Dostoyevsky's *The Devils*; however, in that scene he stands between the cupboard and the wall.

Across the Landing: Casanova's amorous conquests were popular in Russian circles at the beginning of the 20th century. Maria Teresa de Lamballe (1749–1792) was a favourite of Marie Antoinette. In the September uprising of 1792 she was torn to pieces by the mob and her head put on a pike. Maximilian Voloshin wrote a poem about her (1906).

Brocken: the Witches' Sabbath, described by Goethe in *Faust*, happens at Brocken on Midsummer Night, Akhmatova's birthday.

Chapter Two: Columbine: *Commedia dell'arte* stock figure, appears in Blok's play *The Puppet Theatre*.

The Imperial standard (a black eagle on a yellow background) was raised over the Winter Palace when the Tsar was in residence. Tsushima was where the Russian fleet was defeated in the Russo-Japanese war.

The demon: apparently Alexander Blok (as in the poem 'Here Pushkin's exile began', the reference is to Lermontov's poem 'The Demon', with whom the Circassian girl Tamara falls in love), and it is certainly Blok who sends over the black rose in the wine glass – a reference to his poem 'In the Restaurant'.

Chapter Three: The Tsaritsa Avdotya is Eudoxia Lopukhina, the first wife of Peter the Great, the founder of Petersburg, who cursed the city as she was forcibly sent off to be a nun. The Cameron Gallery is at Tsarskoye Selo. This passage is dedicated to N.V. Nedobrovo, Akhmatova's first love.

Chapter Four: The Field of Mars: A large open area between the Summer Garden (still Leningrad's main park), the Mikhailovsky Gardens, and the Neva, used for military parades. Akhmatova lived in the house built by the Adamini brothers from 1924 to 1926. The Cathedral of the Spilt Blood was built on the spot where Tsar Alexander was assassinated in 1881, surrounded on three sides by the Mikhailovsky Gardens.

The Road from Damascus was performed at the Stray Dog. Struve and Filippov note that the 'return' can be either the re-transformation of Paul into Saul, or Olga's return home from the Stray Dog.

Part Two

First Epigraph: 'My future is in my past': The words of Mary Queen of Scots, but marked by Akhmatova as T.S. Eliot – cf. 'Time future is contained in Time past' *(Burnt Norton)* and 'In my beginning is my end' *(East Coker)*.

Second Epigraph: 'The jasmine branch/ where Dante walked and the air is empty.' Akhmatova either had a slightly different version of this poem, or changed *gustoy* (thick) for *pustoy* (empty). I give a lengthy extract from Nikolai

Klyuev's poem 'The Revilers of Art' because Akhmatova said it was the best thing written about her in poetry:

> I am angry with you and I complain from the heart
> that for ten years you never gave
> a handful of oats to the horse of poetry,
> with its diamond-studded bridle, golden-shod hooves
> its saddle-cloth embroidered with harmonies
> or let it out into the field
> where the drunk dew would have refreshed.
> the swan's broken wings.
> The wolf's jaws, the rack, the mines –
> none of these could invent more treacherous tortures
> for the Russian Pegasus in the stone quarry.
> Bats enmeshed themselves in its mane
> and drank its blood, like the dry winds parch the crops,
> so they couldn't ripen to gold,
> and be happily married to the longed-for republic.
>
> ...
> *Akhmatova is a jasmine bush*
> *hemmed in by grey tarmac.*
> *Did she lose her way to the caves*
> *where Dante walked and the air was thick*
> *and a nymph spins crystal flax?*
> Among Russian women, distant Anna
> shines through like a white little cloud
> seen in the evening through the grey willows.

This poem, written in 1932, would seem to tie in Akhmatova's ten year silence with that of the Pegasus of Russian poetry. Akhmatova, in her memoir of Mandelstam, says that she actually saw a statement from Klyuev from labour camp pleading for mercy: 'I am condemned for my poem "The Revilers of Art" and for the crazy lines in my notebooks.' Klyuev was a friend of the immensely popular poet Yesenin.

III: I am conscious that 'dressed up as a milepost', even as fancy dress, does not necessarily work in English. I have counted four or five critics' candidates for this character. Is this what Isaiah Berlin means by saying of *Poem Without a Hero*: 'It is a mysterious and deeply evocative work. A tumulus of learned commentary is inexorably rising over it. Soon it may be buried under its weight.' Akhmatova had plans to write Notes to the Poem on the basis of distracting and leading the reader up various paths.

V: 'soft embalmer' (from Keats' sonnet 'To Sleep') is in English in the original; 'bluebird' is from Maeterlinck's play *L'Oiseau bleu* (1909). 'Elsinore': *Hamlet* (III. 1), 'To sleep, perchance to dream'.

Akhmatova commented: 'the omitted stanzas are an imitation of Pushkin. See also about Evgeny Onegin: "I humbly admit that in *Don Juan* there are two omitted stanzas," Pushkin wrote.' However we do have the omitted verses and it seems right to print these separately from the main text of the Poem, where in "better times" they would have belonged.

> X.
>
> ....
> ....
> ....
> The enemy tortured: come on talk!
> her enemy was to hear no
> groan, no groan or cry...

XI

You ask my contemporaries –
the labour camp women, the martyrs, the prisoners
and we will tell you
how we lived our lives in unconscious terror,
how we raised children for the executioner's
block, the torture chamber and prison.

XII

Clenched our blue lips,
Hecubas driven mad,
Cassandras from Chukhloma,
we will thunder in wordless chorus,
(we, crowned with shame)
'We are on the wrong side of Hell...'

XI: Martyrs: *stopyatnitsy*, literally "one hundred and fivers", the womenfolk who were allowed to live no closer than 105 *vyorsts* from the capitals; also reminiscent of the martyr Paraskeva-Pyatnitsa.

XIV: Luga is a town near Leningrad and 'the land of the satin masks', according to Akhmatova, is Venice. Akhmatova seems to be making a valid psychological development in the attitude to Memory/Mnemosyne. It is fitting that her friend Joseph Brodsky's new book is called *Urania* (the Muse of Astronomy): Dante's *Purgatorio*, Canto XXIX, 'Urania aid me with her choir to put in verse things difficult to think'.

Manfred: Byron's poem of 1817.

Gazoul: alludes to Prosper Merimée's hoax, the *Théâtre de Clara Gazoul*.

Part Three

Parts of this closing section were dedicated to Vladimir Garshin, Akhmatova's doctor friend who stayed behind during the siege of Leningrad. But the main dedication is to the people of Leningrad and the city itself, the city of Pushkin and Dostoyevsky, the city of Akhmatova.

For these Notes I acknowledge my debt to the writing of Amanda Haight, Lydia Chukovskaya, Victor Zhirmunsky, Carl Proffer, Isaiah Berlin, Jessie Davies, articles in *Kontinent* and *Vremya i My* and Anatoly Naiman's valuable work (now published in *Novy Mir*), as well as the help of my Russian friends in London.

Envoi

Anna Akhmatova wrote:

> Our sacred craft has existed
> for thousands of years...
> It is the light of the world even in the darkness.

In 1988 she reached astronomic heights when her name was given to a constellation, newly discovered by Soviet astronomers. Her influence in my own life has been disproportionate to her being 'just a poet'. Time and again she, whom I never knew personally, has been a guiding, guardian angel bringing me to meetings and non-meetings with people; and ultimately leading me to pick up my pen and work on poems that without her I could not have contemplated writing. The relationship is so personal that at times I kept her poems to myself, but hoarding such rich experience and honest experiments in the bottom drawer does not help you, the reader, for whom this book has been compiled. Robert Bly, the American poet and translator, after a reading in London at the end of 1988 said to me: 'We need more Akhmatovas': this, in Akhmatova's 100th anniversary year, is so true it needs no translation.

RICHARD McKANE